Comparative Religion

An Introduction through Source Materials

MICHAEL PYE

Lecturer in Religious Studies,
University of Lancaster

HARPER & ROW, PUBLISHERS
New York Evanston London San Francisco

FIRST UNITED STATES EDITION

STANDARD BOOK NUMBER : 06 – 066715 – x

LIBRARY OF CONGRESS CATALOG CARD NUMBER : 72 – 62220

Contents

Introduction

The purpose of this book is to indicate some of the problems and some of the possibilities in the comparative study of religion which can be illustrated conveniently with extracts from source materials. Some of the extracts included are penetrating and compelling in their own terms, but it should be understood that this is not intended to be an anthology of profound passages of religious writing. Such quasi-theological anthologies already exist in sufficient number.

Nor has a comprehensive survey of all available religions been attempted, with five pages for the greater and two pages for the lesser. Again, such surveys already exist, but they are not necessarily 'comparative' in any significant sense. It is hoped that in a quite incidental way some impression is given here of the variety of different religions, taking seriously those which are major factors in the life of mankind, and avoiding the discrimination which one sometimes finds in western publications between Christianity and 'other' religions.

The book is really meant to be a *systematic* introduction to the *comparative* study of religion, indicating by a series of examples the nature of such a study. The scheme by which the examples are organised, is original, and is explained below. Anybody using this book as a basis for his own study might find it interesting to assemble further materials in terms of the scheme suggested, perhaps introducing greater detail than is possible here, and thinking out some of the problems of categorisation and comparison.

'The comparative study of religion', or 'comparative religion' for short, is really a phrase used to indicate the study of religion in so far as the student is not confining his attentions to a single case-history. It could be argued that every student of religion should be concerned with 'comparative religion' simply because the consideration of data analogous to those with which he is primarily concerned may contribute to his understanding of the latter. Moreover, any general view or theory of religion must take into account the similarities and dissimilarities between specific religions, and hence is dependent on comparative study.

However, one cannot sail happily away into comparative studies without paying attention to serious theoretical problems. Indeed problems are already raised by the very use of such phrases as 'analogous data' and 'general view or theory of religion'. The main theoretical problems which arise can be listed as follows :

1 What data do we wish to treat?
2 What method or methods are appropriate to the data?
3 What may be meant by 'understanding' the data?
4 What may be meant by 'explaining' the data?
5 What may be intended and achieved by 'comparison'?
6 How may the data in general be appropriately organised?
7 What is the nature of further questions which the data themselves raise?

The problems of comparison and organisation of data are perhaps of greatest immediate importance to us, but they cannot be considered in isolation. None of these points can be analysed fully here, but some remarks on each will help to give general orientation to the study.

The extent of the data
The first problem is that of defining the proper object or

objects of the study of religion. This is not so easy as might at first appear. On the one hand there are many items which we might hesitate to include under the concept, eg magic, astrology, divination, veneration of ancestors, yoga, Marxism, psychotherapy, archery, school assemblies, coronation ceremonies, etc. Yet on the other hand some systems generally taken to be 'religious', eg Buddhism, Christianity, Confucianism and Shinto, have sometimes been claimed not to be religions at all. Some clarification is needed here before a consideration of method. It is not possible to discuss in detail the many definitions of religion which have been offered by various writers, or indeed to give detailed justification for a new one. A general warning may not be out of place however: namely that any definition used should not inappropriately distort the field of study from the very start—either by involving unwarranted presumptions about the 'real' nature of religion, or by being so narrowly conceived as to exclude relevant data.

The first danger may be avoided by emphasising the 'operational' nature of the definition required.[1] An 'operational' definition attemps to provide a framework for the study of religion without claiming to define religion normatively or conclusively. It does not attempt to lay bare the 'essence' of religion in any profound sense. It attempts to be precisely not prejudicial with regard to what is 'true' or 'real' religion and what is 'quasi' or 'pseudo' religion. An operational definition of religion does not offer an interpretation of any kind, whether theological, sociological or psychological. Nor should it compete with or seriously conflict with the self-understanding of any particular group of religious persons. In short, the purpose of an operational definition is to obtain a coherent focus upon the subject with as little prejudicial distortion as possible.

Too narrow a definition is usually brought about by selecting a notable characteristic of some one religion or group of religions and universalising it as *the* specific characteristic of all religion. Examples of such inappropriate common denominators are 'belief in spiritual beings',[2] belief in a 'supreme being or god',[3] 'symbolic' reference to 'supernatural values or beings',[4] experience of 'the holy',[5] 'sacred things' in the sense of 'things set apart and forbidden',[6] 'the expression of a dependence',[7] etc. All of these are commonly found among what we may admit to be cases of religion, and yet not one of them seems to be omnipresent. Furthermore, such formulations completely fail to note things which seem to be centrally important in many systems which we should no doubt wish to consider as religions. There are cases, for example, in which the resolution of a fundamental human problem seems to be more important than its conceptual accompaniments, or in which the pursuit of some path of perfection is the overriding interest of those involved. Moreover it is of course not only beliefs which matter, or even beliefs and attitudes or feelings, but also, as various writers have emphasised,[8] the actions of religious people and the groups in which they are associated. To cover these various aspects an appropriate definition must perforce be complex.

Yet however much we may wish to avoid overnarrowness we cannot avoid the question of specificity. Simply to speak of interrelated actions and beliefs, groups of people and states of mind, is obviously not precise enough. We would thereby include a game of poker or a tea-break, or what goes on in a supermarket, as cases of religion, which of course will not do. How can we speak of the specific reference of cases of religion without bringing in concepts from particular religions which distort our general view? One of the most attractive possibilities has been taken up recently by the Japanese writer Kishimoto, who found this specific reference of religion, as distinct from other cultural activities, in the elucidation of 'the ultimate meaning of life' and the 'ultimate solution of its problems'.[9] 'All other cultural institutions', he wrote, 'have only a limited capability. They can express only a relative value of life and give only limited solutions to man's problems. The religious value system stands in distinct contrast to them being believed to have infinite and absolute capability. I call this quality of religion "ultimate".'[10] Mircea Eliade also wrote in similar vein, 'All authentic religious experience' (a problematic phrase!) 'implies a desperate effort to disclose the foundation of things, the ultimate reality.'[11] Others again have drawn on the theology of Paul Tillich and see in his concept of 'ultimate concern' the specific characteristic of religion in general.[12]

However even this reference to the 'ultimate' is not without difficulties. In particular, one wonders whether it is not just a little too far-reaching, too pure, or too profound. Not all persons involved in religion are conscious of any one overriding 'ultimate' concern. In practice, religious beliefs and activities are very mixed, if not confused. They may be more or less 'ultimate' in various circumstances. Not all cases of religion display the terrifying simplicity of Islamic monotheism or the absolutely positionless freedom of Mahayana Buddhism. In attempting to avoid characteristics such as 'spiritual beings' and 'things set apart' we should not allow our specifying characteristic to become more sophisticated than the data in general demand. 'Meaning' is not always 'elucidated', as Kishimoto has it, in religion. 'Meaning' may after all be communicated and grasped almost instinctively in traditional rituals which are never really expounded but only performed. Moreover it is mainly the soteriological religions which attempt to solve problems. For Shinto, say, and perhaps for Islam, life is not really so very problematical. Again it may be argued that certain civic rituals are religious but not of ultimate significance to all the participants. Can we really say that the coronation of the Queen of the United Kingdom of Great Britain and Northern Ireland 'implies a desperate effort to disclose the foundation of things, the ultimate reality'? At the same time, can we deny that it is intended and believed by at least some of the participants to be a significant religious occasion? For these reasons it may be preferable to avoid the near-theological term 'ultimate' and to refer somewhat less dramatically to what the participants take to be fundamentally important aspects of their experience. In this way it is possible to be sufficiently specific in what is intended after all to be no more than an operational definition. It is better, if there is any doubt, that fringe cases should be included as potentially relevant, rather than excluded.

An operational definition may be formulated then as follows : the data for the study of religion are certain sets of actions and concepts together with the social groups and psychological states associated with them; these are located among the generality of sociological and psychological data, but their specific identity lies in their reference to what the persons concerned take to be fundamentally important aspects of their experience. This definition may be presented diagrammatically as below, the circle indicating the interrelatedness and specificity of the four main aspects of the religious phenomenon, and the horizontal axis indicating their location among the generality of sociological and psychological data.

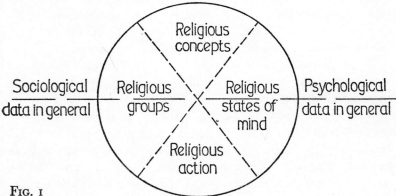

Fig. 1

The simplicity of the diagram is not intended to suggest that religious data are static. For convenience they are often treated as though they were, but in reality they change in time, which means not only that they need to be treated historically, but also that questions arise about the character of religion in motion, so to speak.

Method or methods
If in a preliminary way we have isolated various sets of data

which may appropriately be called 'religious', the question then arises as to how we may try to understand or explain these data. What method or methods are appropriate?

Initially each of the four main aspects of the data can be considered in itself. The most obvious aspect of the study of religion is the painstaking examination of doctrinal systems and credal statements, the contents of holy or authoritative books, and indeed the study of all the myths and legends, laws and histories, symbols and ideas, which play any role in a given religious tradition. This aspect of the study of religion has always been prominent and should continue to be so. After all, unless one has an understanding of what a religion means *to its participants* one cannot really be said to understand it fully. This approach to the data may simply be called the study of religious concepts.

The second line of approach is less obvious at first sight, but arises from the fact that religions are not just doctrines, ideas, myths, and so on, but also involve action. Action should be understood here in a broad sense, ranging from complex festivals and liturgies of various sorts, to meditational exercises, simple isolated actions like making the sign of the cross in a moment of danger, and a whole string of actions 'in the world', so to speak, like 'sweeping a room', which are not obviously religious in themselves but which may be invested with religious or religiously ethical qualities by those who perform them. This second approach may simply be called the study of religious action.

Religious actions are often the actions of a group, and even the apparently isolated actions of individuals cannot really be extracted from their social setting. Religious action, then, and the inseparably related religious concepts, give rise to sociological questions about those involved. We may ask what general statements can be made about the social shape of religion. Similarly, religious actions and concepts give rise to questions about the states of mind of those involved. What general statements can be made about the psychology of individual persons in so far as they are behaving religiously? These questions do not, of course, exhaust the 'sociology' and the 'psychology' of religion, but they are the questions appropriate at this point.

These four main lines of approach are entirely appropriate to the specific character of religion as distinct from, say, economics or art (except in so far as these may themselves be imbued with religious significance). Ideally the four are inseparable, because they deal with different aspects of a set of data which is, in life, an integrated whole. Thus far it is not appropriate to speak of *various* methods in the study of religion; it is better to speak of *the* method with its four main aspects. This integrated approach may be further characterised as 'phenomenological' and 'comparative' as will be explained later. These four essential aspects of the method have been variously assumed and considered by many writers in the past, but it is important to grasp them in a clearcut and integrated manner. They may be represented diagrammatically as follows.

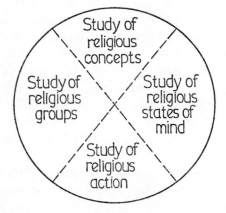

Fig. 2

It was emphasised above that the data of the study of religion are located within the wider generality of human activity and experience both social and individual. This gives rise to further sociological and psychological considerations. How do non-religious factors in society affect the formulation of religious ideas and give shape to religious actions? Conversely can a religion itself be said to influence economic, political and cultural events, and if so in what ways and with what force? Again, how do general psychological factors affect religious ideas and behaviour, and does religion itself influence the inner life of the individual significantly? How is religion related to the whole process of growth and maturation? The psychology of religion has been somewhat neglected recently compared with the sociology of religion, but its importance should not be underestimated.

The essential characteristic of the sociological and psychological approaches as discussed at this point is the correlation of the religious data and other data which are not religious. The study of religious groups and the study of religious states of mind, on the other hand, deal only with data which fall within the circle indicating that which is specifically religious. Thus to bring together these quite diverse approaches under the general terms 'sociology of religion' and 'psychology of religion' might be misleading. The methods brought to bear are quite distinct. At the same time there is clearly some relationship between the study of religious groups and the correlation of religious factors with non-religious social factors; and the same is true of the study of religious states of mind and the correlation of religious factors with non-religious psychological factors. Thus it will be

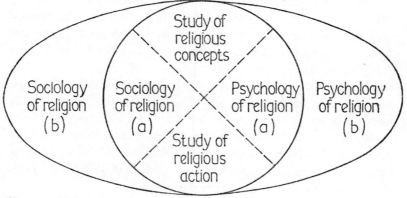

FIG. 3

best to speak of the sociology of religion and the psychology of religion in broad terms, remembering that each has an important subsection which falls within the integrated study of religion as such. These relationships can easily be expressed in terms of a variation of the diagrams used above (see previous page, fig. 3).

'Understanding' the data

If specifically religious data, that is those enclosed within the circle in the above diagrams, are to be studied appropriately, there must be a certain finesse in approach with regard to their meaning. The sense of religious ideas and practices for the believers and practitioners is a crucial consideration. The finesse required may be defined as involving both : (1) a temporary suspension of presuppositions and conclusions about the truth, falsity, value or otherwise of a given set of concepts and actions, and (2) the attempt to elucidate as fully as possible what the concepts, actions, social associations and states of mind mean for the persons involved in them. Theoretically this is simple enough, but the exercise demands experience, patience and skill. These combined requirements form one of the main characteristics of what has been called 'the phenomenological method'. (Two other themes commonly stressed by advocates of this method will be mentioned later.) 'The phenomenological method' has been elaborated in some detail with respect to the study of religion, and with only limited reference to wider philosophical usage of the term 'phenomenology', by writers such as van der Leeuw, Kristensen, Bleeker and Eliade. Van der Leeuw's book *Religion in Essence and Manifestation,* originally published in German in 1933 under the title *Phänomenologie der Religion,* was an early landmark in this development. By systematically attempting to set aside lines of interpretation alien to the subject matter and by trying to be as true as possible to the data as they appear, such writers have been particularly successful in bringing out the meaning of various kinds of symbolism and have contributed much to the 'understanding' of religion.

It is preferable not to speak of 'the phenomenology of religion' as a separate discipline in itself. To do so tends to obscure the fact that the data also lie within the field of sociological and psychological data in general. Those items contained within the circle of specifically religious data are to be studied 'phenomenologically' in the sense given immediately above, and to that extent sociology of religion (a) and psychology of religion (a) are simply subsections of 'the phenomenology of religion'. At the same time the very same data form part of the material for the sociology and the psychology of religion (b). Moreover in either case historical and comparative study is required. Thus the overall approach to the data is complex and the methods must be both distinctive and linked.

Eagerness to assert the necessity and independence of the phenomenological approach has sometimes led to its near isolation. Thus W. B. Kristensen wrote with respect to the phenomenological approach, 'For the historian only one evaluation is possible: "the believers were completely right." '[13] In similiar vein Wilfred Cantwell Smith enunciated the principle 'that no statement about a religion is valid unless it can be acknowledged by that religion's believers.'[14] Yet any set of religious data is enmeshed in a social and psychological context in which the average believer is probably not interested and which he might find very difficult to understand, concerning which indeed it is not inconceivable that he could be wrong. It is therefore necessary to understand not only as the believer understands, but also to approach the wider complexities of the data in a sociological and psychological manner.

'Explaining' the data

Phenomenologists of religion eschew explanations whereas sociologists and psychologists revel in them; and since the work of the three professions is so inextricably related when it comes to the study of religion, one might say that there is a time to explain and a time to refrain from explaining.

When it is time to explain, a distinction may be made between intermediate or partial explanations, which are what are really

B

required in the first instance, and general, conclusive explanations which extend by implication to all religious data. Well-known examples of the latter sort are the Marxist and Freudian theories of religion, each of which purports to explain religion, in general and altogether, in terms of a more fundamental non-religious factor. Briefly stated, religion is, in the first case, the ideological reflection of the economic domination of one social class by another, while in the second case it is seen as the neurotic projection of a father-figure.[15] Leaving aside the question as to whether such theories are empirically justifiable, case by case among the known religions, it is quite clear that either theory entails the view that no religion is true in the way in which its believers understand it to be true. This conflicts with the phenomenological principle enunciated above that as part of our method we are to maintain a temporary suspension of judgement with regard to the truth, falsity, value or otherwise of religious concepts and actions, etc. It is important that this principle should be upheld. That is, in order to proceed fruitfully in the study of religion, one should not assume that the religions in question are *not* true in the way in which their believers believe them to be true, any more than one should assume that they *are* true. Therefore it is necessary also to maintain a temporary methodological suspension of judgement with regard to theories which offer an overall explanation of religion in terms of something else. This argument does not only apply to exhaustive sociological or psychological theories, but also, *mutatis mutandis,* to overall theological explanations such as that men behave religiously because they are seeking after God, or that religions vary because the Buddha uses a variety of means to lead sentient beings to enlightenment. This does not imply that such explanations are ruled out for ever. All it means is that total, definitive explanations should be held at arm's length while the study of religion proceeds. The possibility and the implications of such explanation really belong among the 'further questions which the data themselves raise'.

Intermediate or partial explanations are appropriate as soon as they become feasible. They attempt to draw attention to relationships which seem to exist between religious data in particular and social or psychological factors generally. Of course, partial explanations may also contradict the self-understanding of the participants, but the degree of tension engendered is acceptable because it does not jeopardise the operational framework as a whole. It is usually very difficult to establish the causal direction of such relationships for two reasons. First there is the difficulty of assembling enough individual cases of a similar kind and with sufficiently controllable variables (cf the problem of comparison, below). Secondly there is the difficulty of establishing clear chronological relationships between two sets of factors, say religious and economic, such that dependence of one on the other might reasonably be presumed. Nevertheless it is the desirable and proper task of the sociology and psychology of religion (b) to attempt to establish explanatory relationships of this kind.[16] It is only when such work is naively oversimplified, that the tendency arises persistently and prematurely to explain religious belief and action 'away' altogether in terms of something else.

In terms of the diagrams given above, phenomenological understanding is the intention of work done within the circle of the specifically religious data, while intermediate explanations of a sociological and psychological kind are appropriate to the horizontally extended ellipse.

Comparison

The term 'comparative religion' is somewhat scorned, and properly so, when it is used to refer to rapid and unconnected surveys of the beliefs and practices of a few prominent religions. It has also been criticised by Kristensen on the ground that it implies comparison with a view to making discriminatory value judgements.[17] These undesirable connotations are fairly easy to avoid once they are pointed out.

A greater problem arises from the fact that comparison has also been an integral aspect of 'the phenomenological method' as espoused by van der Leeuw, Bleeker, Eliade, etc, the purpose of it being to contribute to the elucidation of the meaning of 'essence' of the phenomenon 'religion'. This aim was defined carefully above, for present purposes, as the elucidation of what religious concepts, actions, social associations and states of mind mean for the persons involved in them, that is to say, to the specific believers or practitioners concerned. The writers mentioned, however, seem to go beyond this. They wish by means of systematic comparison to seek out the meaning or 'essence' of religion for human beings in general. C. J. Bleeker has written of the phenomenologist of religion. 'His ultimate aim is the inclusive formulation of the essence of religion.'[18] The general assumption seems to be that somehow *behind* the variety of theologies and symbols, rituals and observances, behind the 'manifestations', there waits a deeper meaning or structure, a constantly available 'essence'. This 'essence', the ardent phenomenologist might claim, is instinctively known by the archaically religious person, whereas for disenchanted, modern man it needs to be conjured up again by some creative interpreter. In some cases this approach seems even to have become a substitute for theology. It must of course be admitted here that the data which concern us have sufficient in common for a specific operational definition of religion to be possible. However it seems mistaken to presume that there is an essential inner unity of *meanings* or *meaning,* and to harness the comparative study of the data to the elucidation of that presumed meaning for human beings in general. It may be added that belief in the deeper unity of all religions is itself a well-known theological or dogmatic position characteristic, for example, of the Hindu tradition. This alone should make us beware of turning it into a methodological assumption in the study of religion, which should be free of theological presuppositions of any sort.

Formidable problems for the comparative study of religion are also raised by the diversity of language. Since it is quite impossible for one person to learn more than a small number of languages really well, it might seem more appropriate to restrict one's attention to a limited area such as medieval Hinduism or ancient Germanic religion or early Christianity. However, widespread and interesting facts about religion are now sufficiently well known to force themselves upon our attention, and there seems to be no alternative but that some persons should rely critically on the linguistic expertise of others. Even if this indulgence is granted by the purists there is a more profound problem raised by linguistic diversity. Is it not the case that the meanings of words depend upon the network of language in which they occur, and that the meanings of various religious concepts are therefore delimited altogether by the context of that case of religion in which they occur? For this reason, it might be thought, the comparison of religious concepts as between different cases of religion is strictly impossible. However, religious concepts are only one aspect of the total datum. It soon becomes clear from a survey of materials that religions are not just a string of separate islands in human culture, each of which is utterly different from all others in every possible way. Indeed the very notion of such a string of islands has difficulties of its own, not the least being that as ideas and meanings also differ from time to time within a given cultural context, if these successive moments are to be considered as a random sequence, history itself would become impossible. It seems better to accept the interplay and transmission of ideas as historically real, and also to accept the possibility that people in different places and times spontaneously entertain concepts which are significantly comparable. In short it seems just as inappropriate to presuppose that all religions are utterly different as to presuppose that they are all essentially the same. Thus, as far as religious concepts are concerned there seems to be a justifiable rationale for recent works such as R. C. Zaehner's *Concordant Discord, The Interdependence of Faiths* (Oxford 1971), as also for the rather different approach to the comparison of religious concepts which is taken below.

What then does comparison involve? Simply stated, it involves noting similarities and recurrent associations between relevant data and building these up into theoretical patterns. These theoretical patterns in turn remind us to look for the same characteristics and associations in further cases in which they may lie as yet unnoticed. If the emerging theoretical pattern with respect to some particular aspect of religion proves to be useful it will be retained and developed or modified as necessary, and if not it will be abandoned in favour of another. The comparative study of religion is therefore both more and less than the history of particular religions. On the one hand it is an attempt to begin with data from the history of religions and to go beyond the constraints of the immediate context in order to construct a more generally useful frame of understanding. But on the other hand it is the servant of history and, as a theoretical construct, it always leads back to the attempt to understand particular further cases of religion.[19]

It is very difficult if not impossible to line up several religions which are similar in all important respects, or even to compare all relevant religions in certain respects. In practice it is possible to compare some religions in some respects. Taking the previously used diagram as a base, possible areas of comparison emerge as follows. First it is possible to make a simple comparison of any one of the four main aspects of religious phenomena, that is to say, of religious action, concepts, groups or states of mind. Such comparison does not in itself lead very far, but it does show that there are sufficient substantial similarities between various cases of religion for the work of comparison to be taken seriously. Moreover, experience in making simple comparisons of this sort is an indispensable prerequisite for more complicated assessments, and therefore the sources given below are related first of all to each of these four main aspects of religions in turn (Parts 1-4). Diagrammatically this may be shown as in Figure 4a.

Except in a massive specialised study it is not possible to compare, say, the religious action of various religions in all respects. More commonly the attempt is made to compare some part only of religious action. The comparative study of, say, meditation and prayer, as one part of religious action, may therefore be represented diagrammatically as in Figure 4b.

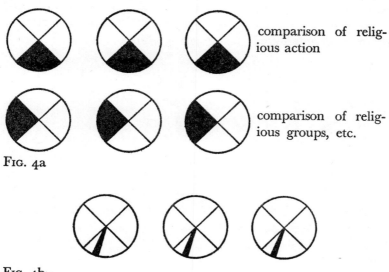

comparison of religious action

comparison of religious groups, etc.

Fig. 4a

Fig. 4b

The subdivisions 1.1, 1.2, 1.3, etc, into which the sources given below are divided, each represent one such segment.

More complex comparisons involve the systematic correlation of two or more of the four basic aspects of religion in some respect or other. This leads at once to extremely complicated problems, and thorough comparability with regard to associations between even just two aspects can only be demonstrated in a substantial detailed study.[20] The cases offered below under the heading 'Complex Comparisons' simply illustrate the possibility of extending the process of comparison to a more complex level. The signficance of what is comparable should not be over-emphasised when what is dissimilar may be equally important. For example, even if certain conceptual and psychological aspects of religion are found to be regularly associated, there may be important sociological aspects which vary from case to case. Or where the social shape of religion seems to fall into some kind of pattern there may be ritual and doctrinal differences which in the long term prove to be significant. If it were not too clumsy it might be preferable to speak of 'the comparative and contrastive study of religion'. These complex comparisons may be represented in terms of the diagram as follows:

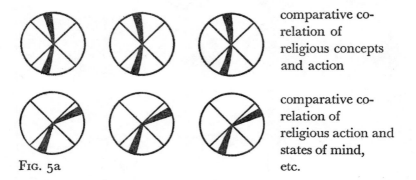

comparative co-relation of religious concepts and action

comparative co-relation of religious action and states of mind, etc.

Fig. 5a

The four main aspects of religion may be correlated along these lines in eleven different ways, and these form the subdivisions of Part 5 below.

So far the elaboration has been made in terms of the four main aspects circumscribed by the circle in the diagrams, and to this must now be added the wider sociological and psychological setting. This means that the area to be studied comparatively is not coterminous with the area to be studied phenomenologically, but extends beyond it. Since a variety of non-religious factors may be related to any of the four main aspects of the religious data as such, either singly or in combination, comparative work becomes very complicated indeed. Parts 6 and 7 below by no means offer an introduction to the sociology and psychology of religion in any detail, but they indicate the kind of questions raised in these fields. The materials given there are brief and elementary, but to have omitted them altogether would have meant giving a quite distorted picture of what the comparative study of religion is about. Diagrammatically this further area of comparison may be represented, for example, as in Figure 5b.

Finally it should be remembered, with regard to all that has been said above, that religions should not be considered only as

FIG. 5b

static phenomena. Religions 'in motion' are just as deserving of study, and thus of comparative study, as are the 'stills' which have hitherto been given undue prominence. The historical reasons for the relative neglect of the 'dynamics' of religion (to use van der Leeuw's term) may be obscure,[21] but whatever they may be they ought now to be exorcised. This dimension of religion needs attention with respect to all four major aspects of the data as well as in the wider sociological and psychological context. It may be possible to discern some relationship between social or psychological factors and theological atrophy or renewal, or between the nature and intensity of religious action and the speed of doctrinal change. The sociological study of new religious movements may raise the question of when it is appropriate to describe a religion as 'new', which in turn raises questions about tradition and authority, interpretation and reinterpretation, leading and accessory characteristics, etc. This leads on to many of the questions considered important by the intellectual practitioners of religion, the theologians, buddhologians, etc. The 'dynamics' of religion are not treated separately below, but they are held in view whenever it seems appropriate.

Organisation of the data

How to organise the data in our minds is a problem which emerges naturally out of the methodological questions considered above. The four main aspects of specifically religious data, their place among more general factors and the variously articulated method appropriate to their study are all threads which help us organise the data in a manner which cuts across and goes beyond separate histories of religions. This is not to say that histories of religions are unimportant. They are the basis from which the theoretical patterns of comparative study arise and to which they return. Even a general history of religion is theoretically possible and has been attempted by various writers, although there is clearly room for discussion about what such a general history should be like. It is interesting to compare, for example, the recent books by Ninian Smart and Trevor Ling, entitled *The Religious Experience of Mankind* and *A History of Religion East and West* respectively, which, while written for a wide readership, show awareness of the methodological problems involved. Nevertheless the data must also be organised in a theoretical and a historical fashion, and here too various attempts have been made in the past, especially by writers associated with 'the phenomenological school'. These attempts cannot be examined in detail, but four general points need to be stressed.

First the organisation of the data has often proceeded on the basis of an unbalanced presentation of the main aspects of religion. Van der Leeuw, for example, in *Religion in Essence and Manifestation*, has an extremely wide and varied mass of data organised almost entirely in terms of selected religious concepts. Kristensen's *The Meaning of Religion* divides religion into three areas, namely 'religious cosmology', 'religious anthropology' and 'cultus', the first two being conceptual and the third referring to a part only of religious action as a whole. Eliade's *Patterns in Comparative Religion* (1958) and his survey of materials in *From Primitives to Zen* (1963) are both organised almost entirely in terms of a variety of religious concepts. In the latter case miscellaneous forms of religious action are scattered throughout the book and there is no clear attempt to deal with religious groups and religious states of mind. Against this trend it should be stressed that the wish to treat the beliefs of religious people seriously, or more precisely, phenomenologically, should not lead us too quickly into classifying the data only or mainly in terms of those beliefs.

Perhaps the nearest to the ideal is Joachim Wach's arrangement in *The Comparative Study of Religions* (1958), a book which represents the final state of his thinking on the subject. After a chapter on methodology the main part of this work consists of four chapters—'The Nature of Religious Experience', 'The Expression of Religious Experience in Thought', 'The Expression of Religious Experience in Action' and 'The Expression of Religious Experience in Fellowship'. The last three of these correspond roughly to three of the four main aspects delineated above. The drawback remains that the first, 'The Nature of Religious Experience', is somewhat anomalous. The other three are seen as the 'expression' of this 'nature'.[22] In the first, Wach is not concerned with the study of religious states of mind in a manner which would be complementary to his discussion of 'The Expression of Religious Experience in Fellowship'. Rather the idea behind it is that 'In opposition to the popular preoccupation with the quest for the function of religion it is necessary to stress the search for the nature of religion.'[23] In effect therefore Wach is using this chapter to maintain the integrity of specifically religious data among socio-psychological data generally. It is an over-eager and misplaced reaction to the threat of reductionist explanation. The response to this threat, as explained above, should be to treat religious data phenomenologically as well as sociologically and psychologically, and to hold over the possibility of comprehensive explanation in non-religious terms as a problem which lies beyond the scope of the immediately appropriate method. Wach, by reacting as he does, tangles up a discussion of 'the nature' of religious experience and the consideration of religious states of mind as one aspect of it, thus distorting the overall balance which he almost achieved. In reality 'religious experience' cannot be isolated into any one corner of the total religious datum, but it is rather the believer's or the practitioner's involvement at one and the same time in religious concepts, action, groups and states of mind.

The general organisation of the data, then, should attempt to hold a balance between these four main aspects without making any one the master of the others. As it happens, it seems necessary to speak of precisely these four. To subcategorise further at this primary level is to introduce unnecessary complications, while to omit any one is to introduce significant distortion. These four aspects therefore should prove to be a stable and permanent element in any organisation of religious data.

The second point to be stressed is that the location of these four main aspects of religious data within the wider context of sociological and psychological fact should not be forgotten. Too often there has been a complete separation of the 'phenomenology' of religion from the 'sociology' and the 'psychology' of religion. These are admittedly distinguishable but also interrelated, and the comparative study of religion involves them all. Of course, not everything can be considered at once in detail. However the phenomenological study of religious action, concepts, groups and states of mind, that is to say, of the fundamental aspects of religious experience of which the believer is himself aware, cannot be isolated in principle from an interest in concomitant sociological and psychological factors of which the believer is probably unaware. Conversely, works on the sociology or psychology of religion which completely ignore the phenomenological approach to the meaning of the data for the participants do so at their peril. It may be held that on the whole the writings of 'the phenomenological school' have been too isolationist in this regard; although Wach, for example, made an integrated study of religious groups and non-religious social factors in his *Sociology of Religion,* while the works of van der Leeuw and of Eliade are partially though confusedly infiltrated by psychological theories.

Thirdly the organisation of the data must not be bedevilled by theological assumptions about the nature or meaning of religion. Positively stated, the data should continue to be delimited 'operationally', thus leaving open further questions about the 'essential' nature or 'ultimate' meaning of religion. Of course the data *could* be organised on the basis of some evaluative or normative standpoint, theological or other. However, we are now concerned with the elaboration of a generally valid, operational scheme for

the organisation of the data. The purpose of a theologically con-
ditioned arrangement would be to articulate the data in a manner
consonant with the postulates of the theological system concerned, for apologetic or other reasons. The purpose of a
neutrally developed organisation of the data is to provide a
coherent framework for further progress in their study. Such an
arrangement is to be tested then, not by checking off its agreement with theological (or similar) criteria, but by its appropri-
ateness to the continuously emergent data themselves.

In this respect van der Leeuw's *Religion in Essence and
Manifestation* is again unsatisfactory, not so much because it is
consciously theological, which in its own way would be perfectly
acceptable, but because while claiming to be non-theological he
fails to be operationally neutral. For example, although he
attempted to neutralise the polar Christian categories of God
and man, he actually revamped them as 'the object of religion'
and 'the subject of religion'. These two concepts cover the first
two parts of his work, while the third was entitled 'Object and
Subject in Reciprocal Relation'. The game is finally given away
in the last section entitled 'The Mediator', which clearly reflects
the importance of soteriology and indeed of christology in
Christian dogmatics. Here comparative religion becomes apolo-
getics, and when we reach 'the borderland of phenomenology'
it is the *Christian* revelation before which 'the contemplative
and comprehending servant of research' must stop short.[24]
Kristensen, too, followed the same basic pattern in his *The
Meaning of Religion*. What, after all, are 'religious cosmology',
'religious anthropology' and 'cultus' if not cyphers for God, man
and the relationship between the two? The assumption that this
is the essential shape of religion dominates the shape of his whole
work. In contrast to such unconsciously prejudicial approaches,
an arrangement in terms of the four main aspects, linked also
with the wider sociological and psychological setting, may both
maintain the phenomenological integrity of the data, and display no favouritism with regard to any particular religious
tradition.

Fourthly there is the question of how far it is possible to rely on categories drawn from the religions themselves when articulating the data in greater detail. Again, van der Leeuw's procedure is a good example of what is not appropriate. He began first with the notion of 'power', working it out on the basis of Codrington's famous report on the Melanesian concept of *mana*. Other parts of his work, however, are completely dominated by various aspects of the idea of God, which are obviously drawn straight from the Christian tradition. The section on 'Inward Action', for example, has the following subheadings: 'Religious Experience, The Avoidance of God, Servitude to God, The Covenant with God, Friendship with God, Knowledge of God, The Following of God, Being Filled with God, Mysticism, The Love of God, Children of God, Enmity to God, Conversion, Rebirth, Faith, Adoration.' It would be an interesting exercise to begin again and write this list in Buddhist terms.

Some terms can indeed be straightforwardly applied in a variety of contexts. One thinks for example of 'reformer', 'myth', 'scripture' and so on. Others again are problematic. How far is it appropriate to extend the use of words such as 'prophet', 'guru', 'shaman', 'priest', 'sacrifice', 'worship', 'prayer' or 'mantra'? On the one hand it seems best to keep to their original field of reference words like 'shaman' which conjure up a particular range of religious data. On the other hand it is perhaps precisely *across* the borders of linguistic history that comparisons may most usefully be made. Is the ninefold *kyrie* best understood as a 'prayer' or as a 'mantra'? Such dilemmas constantly confront the would-be organiser of religious data. There always has to be the neutral generality of the four main aspects of religious data, yet detailed particulars need to be considered in terminology appropriate to themselves. In this area of subcategorisation there is yet much scope for diversity of judgement. Indeed if overall organisation can be agreed, secondary organisation and nomenclature are really pressing methodological problems in the study of religion, and ought to become matters of careful international discussion.

It may perhaps be agreed that the arrangement of the sources below satisfactorily meets the first three of these points about the organisation of the data. That is to say, the primary problems of organisation may be said to be solved, in the sense that any set of data which one might conceivably wish to consider under the general notion of religion can be examined in terms of the arrangement given, without any difficulty or strain. But it must be admitted that only a few preliminary steps have been taken towards solving the many problems of subcategorisation.

Further questions

The kind of question referred to now really falls outside the scope of the study of religion if it is defined strictly as above. However, since they are questions which are raised by the data themselves it is impossible to exclude them from methodological considerations. Nor is there any reason why they should not be treated within the field of the study of religion more broadly defined, as in universities and schools. It is simply that they are questions which in various ways go beyond the competence of the method delimited above, and they are not specifically catered for in the arrangement of sources below. The position of these questions may be represented on the basis of the earlier diagram as in Figure 6. See next page.

Questions of truth, falsity, value or otherwise may be raised when we purposely abandon the method appropriate to the phenomenological circle. We may wish to examine the inner consistency of a belief system from a critical point of view, or to assess its consistency with our own manner of understanding the world, or its consistency or manner of conflict with the views of some philosopher or with the generality of scientific thinking in the world. We may wish to consider what kind of criteria might be appropriate for testing or evaluating the statements made by religious persons. Or we may wish to embark on the systematic formulation of value judgements.[25]

A specially thorny question is whether the phenomenological elucidation of meanings and values for believers does not lead

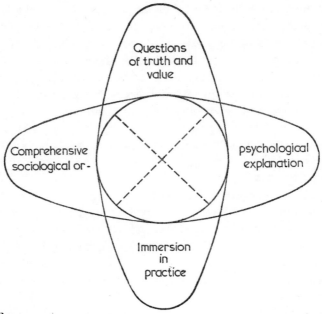

FIG. 6

inexorably on, all protestations notwithstanding, to the statement of meanings for the student himself or for the wider world. Can meanings be elucidated at all without interpretation? If a degree of interpretation is necessarily involved in the second-hand elucidation of meaning, is the elucidator not thereby contributing to the developing meaning of the religious tradition in question, even though he professes suspense with regard to any religious claim or stance on his own part? This is a dilemma in the study of religion which needs continuously to be made explicit. Once exposed the problem can be resolved by the application of Cantwell Smith's criterion already referred to. That is, in so far as the elucidation made by the student can, at least in principle, be checked against and confirmed by avowed practitioners of the religion in question, the student remains within the phenomenological circle. If, however, he develops meanings in such a way that they go beyond what the practitioners themselves may reasonably be claimed to mean, then he must be said either to have strayed or to have ventured beyond the phenomenological circle into the realm of questions about the wider meaning of religion for men in general. It could probably be argued that the work of Eliade frequently does just this. To extend the meaning of the data in this way is not necessarily bad, but it is important to be clear about what is being done.

The dynamic aspects of religion bring one particularly close to this particular razor's edge. The student has a detached perspective in which to see the work of intellectual practitioners of various religions, yet he is also led by his method very near to the heart-beat of their creative and interpretative efforts. Questions such as 'Can Christianity be demythologised?', 'What is the essence of Buddhism?', 'What is the importance of the classical writers in the Marxist tradition?' or 'What criteria should be applied in the application of Muslim law to contemporary conditions?' are most appropriately answered by practitioners of the religions concerned. However, since the questions and the various answers given to them are themselves part of the data of religion, the student is confronted with them again and again. It may even be that, although he is not an officially authorised interpreter of any one of these traditions, he is able to use his organised understanding of religious data to contribute to the solution of some contemporary problems.

The comparative aspect of the method also raises various questions of truth. To take a simple example, if we note the multiplicity of stories about the miraculous births of founders of religions, it becomes impossible to take a naïve view about the unique meaning of any one. Again, the frequency of appeal to revelation in support of various claims about religious truth which themselves conflict makes it impossible for any rational man to accept one of these claims on the ground of revelation alone. This does not mean that it is irrational to accept a 'revelation'. It may simply suggest that accepting 'it' (whatever 'it' is, which is usually a problem in itself) 'because it is revealed'

C

is really a rationalisation made after the real acceptance has already taken place for more profound 'reasons'. The comparative study of religion may lead us therefore to study those more profound reasons and perhaps even to seek new criteria of evaluation altogether.

The prospect of giving a comprehensive explanation of religion in sociological or psychological terms, or in a combination of both (the horizontal ellipse in the diagram), will no doubt always tantalise those who find serious difficulties in the way of accepting any known religious system in its own terms. There is no reason why such theories should not be taken very seriously. Moreover, while they should not be allowed to distort the generally shared on-going methodology, since none has yet been shown to be conclusively and comprehensively satisfactory, it may be that detailed work in the field will affect the formulation and viability of comprehensive socio-psychological theories.

Similarly there is no reason why religious theories of the nature and meaning of religion (upper extension of circle, with other questions of truth and value) should not be taken seriously. Such theories arise from reflection on the data by the intellectual practitioners of various religions, and they can also be studied phenomenologically and comparatively themselves as is done briefly in 4.10 below. The question raised here, however, is whether any one such theory is in fact true or compelling. As in the case of the socio-psychological theories, a shift in the understanding of the detailed data may have some effect on overall theories of this kind. That is, it may have some effect on the attitude of a particular practitioner towards religion in general and even to a shift in his understanding of his own religion or 'religious position'.

The vertical ellipse in the diagram makes its downward extension in the direction of religious action. This indicates the possibility of abandoning altogether the suspense involved in persistently carrying on the study of religious data with the method appropriate to them, and taking up instead the practice of some religious action such as doing *zazen* or joining the Salvation Army. Strictly speaking it has yet to be demonstrated that suspense and commitment in the senses required are incompatible. However, the point is that many who do take the course of 'practice' do themselves feel that they are escaping from the snares of intellectualism. While this 'question' may be a little different from the other 'questions' above, it should nevertheless be noted, analogously, that advance in the understanding of religions by the method appropriate to the data may raise issues of importance for purist practitioners. For example, a clear understanding of the manner in which utopian religious communities rise, flourish and wither might be of great interest to somebody who is on the brink of joining one.

Such then are the 'further questions' which arise in the study of religion. Many of them have for long been studied as problems in the philosophy of religion, theology, sociology and so on, and they should by no means be ignored in the future. For the sake of clarity, however, it is useful to reorganise them as being 'further questions' from the point of view of the systematic comparative study of religion as defined earlier. If this distinction can be observed there is no reason why, say, a Moslem, a Marxist and a Buddhist should not be able to co-operate in the comparative study of religion, while at the same time the questions which each respectively considers to be of great importance will undoubtedly be raised. For this to be possible it is essential that the neutralised working methodological framework be stabilised and maintained, at least in a provisional sense, and for this reason a little space has been devoted to it here.

PART ONE

Religious Action

Religious action is repeated or sustained action
following what is normally an authoritative pattern. It is of course intimately related to
the religious concepts apart from which it could
only with difficulty be characterised as specifically religious.
This means that it can only with difficulty be treated apart from
these. Indeed a proper understanding of religious action should
involve the recognition not only of significant conceptual variations associated with it but also of social and psychological
differences which may emerge from case to case. At the same
time religious action alone does seem to be genuinely comparable over a wide area, and as a first step only this comparability
is illustrated in the sources which follow.

There are two problems about the subsidiary categorisation
of religious action. The first is that even the ten broadly conceived types of action detailed below frequently overlap with
each other. For example, a complex religious event such as a
Christian Eucharist service might be held to involve not only
special times, places and objects, but also purification and
separation, sacrifice and worship, the rehearsal of myth or of the
significant past, and meditation and prayer. Unfortunately, if we
are going to organise and categorise the data of religion at all,
in order to seek initial points of comparability between different
cases, such dismemberment is inevitable. This need not affect
our ability to appreciate the meaning of such a complex event
as a larger whole.

The second problem is that the precise meanings of various cases of religious action, such as those just mentioned, vary importantly in accordance with the theological standpoint of the Church in question and the beliefs of its members at various times. Of course the precise meanings for practitioners will vary even more widely between different religions. It might be preferable therefore not to use *any* religious terms, such as 'sacrifice', to indicate general categories of religious action. Nevertheless in the absence of a generally understood neutral terminology it is necessary to do so. The dangers of using terms which have specific significance in specific religious contexts may be minimised by using two or three in association. For example, 'meditation' and 'prayer' are associated because it is possible to descry here a broadly coherent type of religious activity. Such a field should not at this point be subdivided arbitrarily in terms of whether or not the practitioners believe the activity to be directed towards a being significantly other than themselves. That is to say that prayers to Allah, Hindu mantras and Buddhist meditation are both various and comparable, and at this point we are interested in the comparability.

For such reasons the categorisation which follows is very broadly intended. The intention to indicate no more than the general comparability of the main aspects of religious action should be carefully noted or false conclusions may be drawn.

1.1 SPECIAL PLACES, TIMES AND OBJECTS

Attention to special, or 'holy', places, times and objects is perhaps the most obvious type of religious action. The fact that it is not the only type or that it may be in some way problematical is often emphasised by religious persons themselves (cf 5.1).

The obvious similarities in this area have led to some

massive comparative essays such as Mircea Eliade's *Patterns in Comparative Religion*, though even these are by no means exhaustive. Care should be taken that comparability of function between selected examples is not too quickly presumed to imply a common underlying meaning. The examples adduced below are comparable precisely with regard to the role of special places, times and objects within religious action. They are drawn from contexts offering widely divergent meanings.

1.1.1 Pilgrimage in Buddhism

And there will come, Ânanda, to such spots, believers, brethren and sisters of the Order, or devout men and devout women, and will say:—'Here was the Tathâgata born!' or, 'Here did the Tathâgata attain to the supreme and perfect insight!' or 'Here was the kingdom of righteousness set on foot by the Tathâgata!' or, 'Here the Tathâgata passed away in that utter passing away which leaves nothing whatever to remain behind!'

And they, Ânanda, who shall die while they, with believing heart, are journeying on such pilgrimage, shall be reborn after death, when the body shall dissolve, in the happy realms of heaven. T. W. and C. A. F. Rhys Davids. *Dialogues of the Buddha* Part II (1910, 1966), 154 (*Mahâ Parinibbâna Suttanta* V 8)

Tathâgata is a common name for the Buddha. Rebirth in one of the heavens is a lesser achievement than Nirvana itself.

1.1.2 The remains of the Tathâgata

And as they treat the remains of a king of kings, so, Ânanda, should they treat the remains of the Tathâgata. At the four crossroads a cairn should be erected to the Tathâgata. And whosoever shall there place garlands or perfume or paint, or make salutation there, or become in its presence calm in heart—that shall long be to them for a profit and a joy. Rhys Davids. *Dia-*

logues of the Buddha Part II, 156 (*Mahâ Parinibbâna Suttanta*
V 11)

1.1.3 The Black Stone

The blessed Black Stone is enchased in the corner facing east.
The depth to which it penetrates it is not known, but it is said
to extend two cubits into the wall. Its breadth is two-thirds of a
span, its length one span and a finger joint. It has four pieces,
joined together, and it is said that it was the Qarmata [Carma-
thians]—may God curse them—who broke it. Its edges have
been braced with a sheet of silver whose white shines brightly
against the black sheen and polished brilliance of the Stone, pre-
senting the observer a striking spectacle which will hold his looks.
The Stone, when kissed, has a softness and moistness which so
enchants the mouth that he who puts his lips to it would wish
them never to be removed. This is one of the special favours of
Divine Providence, and it is enough that the Prophet—may God
bless and preserve him—declare it to be a covenant of God on
earth. May God profit us by the kissing and touching of it. By
His favour may all who yearn fervently for it be brought to it.
J. R. C. Broadhurst (trans). The Travels of Ibn Jubayr (1952), 85

Ibn Jubayr made a pilgrimage from Spain to Mecca between
1183 and 1185.

1.1.4 The fast of Ramadan

Ramadan is the month in which was revealed the Quran, which
is a perfect guidance for mankind and which consists of such
clear teachings as show the right way and are a criterion of
Truth and falsehood. Therefore from now on whoever witnesses
it, he shall have to fast the whole month. And if anyone be ill
or on a journey, he should make up that same number by fasting on other days. Allah desires to show leniency to you and not
hardship. Hence this way is being shown to you so that
you may make up that number of fast days and glorify Allah for
the Guidance He has shown to you and be grateful to Him.

Abul A'la Maududi, *The Meaning of the Quran* (Lahore 1967), 129 (surah ii, 185)

1.1.5 The Sabbath

Observe the Sabbath day, to keep it holy, as the Lord your God commanded you. Six days you shall labour, and do all your work; but the seventh day is a sabbath to the Lord your God; in it you shall not do any work, you, or your son, or your daughter, or your manservant, or your maidservant, or your ox, or your ass, or any of your cattle, or the sojourner who is within your gates, that your manservant and your maidservant may rest as well as you. You shall remember that you were a servant in the land of Egypt, and the Lord your God brought you out thence with a mighty hand and an outstretched arm; therefore the Lord your God commanded you to keep the sabbath day. Deuteronomy v, 12-15

Cf Exodus xx, 8-11, where the sabbath is related to the seventh day after the six days of creation, on which God rested.

1.1.6 A pilgrimage to Peking

Then innumerable red flags were fluttering in the wind in front of The Gate of Heavenly Peace. The Young Pioneers came by in ranks and made a *dong dong* sound with their drums. They held up fresh flowers and called out : 'A long life to the Communist Party ! A long life to Chairman Mao !'

Today was indeed national celebration day.

Many, many balloons floated up and danced happily high in the sky. Chairman Mao, up on The Gate of Heavenly Peace, nodded and smiled at them. Zi Mang Zhong. *Fei Dao Tian An Men Qu* (Peking 1966), 23

This is the climax of a children's story about a red balloon, which makes what is in effect a pilgrimage across China to the great festival at Peking.

———

1.2   THE USE OF THE BODY

The precise control of posture and breathing in yoga, meticulous body movements in social relationships and the taking up of varied positions in worship and devotion are all examples of the importance attached to the use of the body in religious situations. Mention should also be made of systematic self-mortification (cf 3.2) as opposed to mere bodily control, and also of religious dance (cf 5.4).

1.2.1   Posture and breathing

We have the following to say of the postures and other [aids to yoga]. In this [sūtra, it is said]—

Stable-and-easy posture

For example, the lotus-posture and the hero-posture and the decent-posture and the mystic diagram and the staff-posture and [the posture] with the rest and the bedstead, the seated curlew and the seated elephant and the seated camel, the even arrangement, the stable-and-easy—also called, as-is-easiest—and others of the same kind . . .

When there is this [stability of posture], *the restraint of breath cutting off the flow of inspiration and expiration* [follows].

After the mastery of posture [follows the restraint of the breath]. Inspiration is the sipping in of the outer wind; expiration is the expulsion of the abdominal wind. Restraint of the breath is the cutting off of the flow of these two, the absence of both kinds. James Haughton Woods (trans). *The Yoga-system of Patañjali*. Harvard Oriental Series XVII (1914, Delhi 1966), 191-3

The extract contains both Patañjali's text (italicised), which alone is barely comprehensible, and the commentary attributed to Veda-vyāsa.

1.2.2   Posture, dress and food

On entering the duke's gateway he would bow as though there

were not room to remain upright. He would not stand in the doorway; he would not step on the threshold as he entered. As he passed by the prince's empty place, his countenance would change and his step become uncertain; his speech became like a dumb man's. As he mounted with lifted skirt to the audience hall he seemed to be making a bow; he held his breath as if unable to breathe. On leaving, as soon as he had descended one ,step, he looked pleased. From the bottom of the steps he moved quickly forward, his arms extended in such a way as to make one think of a bird's wings. On returning to his own place at the reception he became respectful to an extreme degree . . .

On receiving a man in mourning, even though a close friend, he would assume an appropriate air. When receiving an official or a blind man, even though he knew him very well, he would assume an appropriate attitude . . .

When getting into his carriage he held himself erect and grasped the rope firmly. Once in the carriage he did not peer around; he did not shout; he did not point. James R. Ware (trans). *The Sayings of Confucius* (New York 1955), 65-9 X. 3 etc)

This model of sustained, disciplined decorum in the minute matters of daily life and personal relations has had a long-lasting influence in the Far East.

1.2.3 Postures in worship

And although the keeping or omitting of a Ceremony, in itself considered, is but a small thing; yet the wilful and contemptuous transgression and breaking of a common order and discipline is no small offence before God . . .

The Table, at the Communion-time having a fair white linen cloth upon it, shall stand in the body of the Church, or in the Chancel . . . And the Priest standing at the north side of the Table shall say the Lord's Prayer, with the Collect following, the people kneeling. *Book of Common Prayer* (1662). Opening sentence taken from 'Of Ceremonies, why some be abolished, and some retained', then the first rubric of the whole series in 'The order of the administration of the Lord's Supper or Holy Communion'

1.3 SEPARATION AND RITUAL CLEANSING

Innumerable religious actions have been devised to separate what is 'holy' or 'clean' from what is 'profane' or 'unclean' and a full discussion could cover many cases which are only loosely interrelated. For example, special places or objects are often marked off by some special symbol such as a gate, fence or steps. Or one might turn to the many codes of prohibitions and allowances relating to eating habits and many other aspects of daily life. Many examples of separation and cleansing are undoubtedly based on the very practical need to isolate disease or its sources, as in some of the examples below, but the notions of holiness and of ritual cleanness, even of moral cleanness, are usually evidenced as well. The use of water as a symbolic cleanser is very widespread indeed.

1.3.1 Preservation of sacred elements from pollution

O Maker of the material world, thou Holy One! If a man shall throw on the ground the whole body of a dead dog, or of a dead man, and if grease or marrow flow from it on to the ground, what penalty shall he pay?

Ahura Mazda answered: 'A thousand stripes with the Aspahê-astra, a thousand stripes with the Shraoshô-*k*arana.'

O Maker of the material world, thou Holy One! If a worshipper of Mazda, walking, or running, or riding, or driving, come upon a corpse in a stream of running water, what shall he do?

Ahura Mazda answered: 'Taking off his shoes, putting off his clothes, boldly, O Zarathustra! he shall enter the river, and take the dead out of the water; he shall go down into the water ankle-deep, knee-deep, waist-deep, or a man's full depth, till he can reach the dead body . . . He shall draw out of the water as much of the corpse as he can grasp with both hands, and he shall lay it down on the dry ground; no sin attaches to him for any bone, hair, grease, flesh, dung, or blood that may drop back into the water.' . . .

O Maker of the material world, thou Holy One! If worshippers of Mazda, walking, or running, or riding, or driving, come upon a corpse-burning fire, whereon a corpse is being cooked or roasted, what shall they do?

Ahura Mazda answered: 'They shall kill the man that burns the corpse; surely they shall kill him . . .'

O Maker of the material world, thou Holy One! Whither shall we bring, where shall we lay the bodies of the dead, O Ahura Mazda?

Ahura Mazda answered: 'On the highest summits, where they know there are always corpse-eating dogs and corpse-eating birds, O holy Zarathustra! . . .' James Darmesteter (trans). *The Zend-Avesta, Part I, The Vendīdād*. Max Müller (ed). Sacred Books of the East IV (1880, Delhi 1956), 69-70, 110-1 and 72-3

According to this ancient Iranian scripture the sacred elements, earth, water and fire, are not to be polluted by death; hence the specialised funeral custom which is still followed by the Parsees in India. Specially built platforms raised off the ground were gradually refined into very complex and exact structures (cf Modi, *The Religious Ceremonies and Customs of the Parsees* (Bombay 1937), 67-70)

1.3.2 Purification after contact with death

Thereafter, Izanagi no Mikoto went after Izanami no Mikoto, and entered the land of Yomi. When he reached her they conversed together, and Izanami no Mikoto said : 'My lord and husband, why is thy coming so late? I have already eaten of the cooking-furnace of Yomi. Nevertheless I am about to lie down to rest. I pray thee, do not thou look on me.' Izanagi no Mikoto did not give ear to her, but secretly took his many-toothed comb and, breaking off its end tooth, made of it a torch, and looked at her.

Putrefying matter had gushed up, and maggots swarmed . . .
Izanagi no Mikoto was greatly shocked, and said : 'Nay! I have
come unawares to a hideous and polluted land.' So he speedily
ran away back again . . .

When Izanagi no Mikoto had returned, he was seized with
regret, and said, 'Having gone to . . . a hideous and filthy place,
it is meet that I should cleanse my body from its pollutions.' He
accordingly went to the plain of Ahagi at Tachibana in Wodo in
Hiuga of Tsukushi, and purified himself. When at length he was
about to wash away the impurities of his body, he lifted up his
voice and said, 'The upper stream is too rapid and the lower
stream is too sluggish.' So he washed in the middle stream. The
God which was thereby produced was called Ya-so-maga-
tsu-bi no Kami, and then to remedy these evils there were produced Deities named Kami-nawo-bi no Kami, and after him
Oho-nawo-bi no Kami. W. G. Aston (trans). *Nihongi, Chronicles
of Japan from the Earliest Times to A.D. 697* (1896, 1956), 24,
26-7

Izanagi and Izanami are the male and female procreative deities.
Izanami died at the birth of the Fire-God and went to the land
of the dead, Yomi. The names of the gods produced in the purification are based on words meaning 'eighty-evils-of-body' and
'remedy'. Various details of the myth have parallels elsewhere.
Though this myth itself predates the entry of Buddhism into
Japan, the latter religion has for centuries offered a funeral service there, leaving Shinto to content itself with the brighter side
of life.

1.3.3 The ritual cleansing of lepers

The Lord said to Moses, 'This shall be the law of the leper for the
day of his cleansing. He shall be brought to the priest; and the
priest shall go out of the camp, and the priest shall make an
examination. Then, if the leprous disease is healed in the leper,
the priest shall command them to take for him who is to be
cleansed two living clean birds and cedarwood and scarlet stuff

and hyssop; and the priest shall command them to kill one of the birds in an earthen vessel over running water. He shall take the living bird with the cedarwood and the scarlet stuff and the hyssop, and dip them and the living bird in the blood of the bird that was killed over the running water; and he shall sprinkle it seven times upon him who is to be cleansed of leprosy; then he shall pronounce him clean, and let the living bird go into the open field . . .' Leviticus xiv. 1-7

This is only part of a long passage in which there is a clear emphasis on ritual cleanness as well as the actual cure.

1.3.4 Purification at a morning bath

I seek the Lord of Waters [Varuṇa] whose surface is golden; entreated by us, give me a ford [for bathing and purifying myself]; the food I have eaten at the house of bad people, the gift I have received from evil men, the sin I have committed with my mind, by word or deed; of all that may Indra, Varuṇa, Bṛihaspati, and Sun purify me again and again. The sin of overeating, overdrinking, and receiving [gifts] from people of violent ways, may King Varuṇa wipe it off with his hand. Let me thus, rid of evil, impurity, and sin become liberated, ascend to heaven and attain the world of the Lord of creation. Kenneth W. Morgan (ed). *The Religion of the Hindus* (New York 1953), 291 (*Taittirīya Āraṇ yaka* X.i)

Bṛihaspati is a deity who intercedes with other gods on behalf of worshippers.

1.4 SACRIFICE, OFFERING AND WORSHIP

These terms, once again, refer to a whole complex of activities which cannot be easily surveyed but which all have in common the ritual presentation of a gift of some kind. The gift is not necessarily thought to be of any real value in itself to the presumed recipient, though it may be of very great importance to the giver. The intention may vary from atonement for sin to the achievement of positive merit in some spiritual path; or again it may be meant as a thanksgiving, or it may mark in some other way the natural cycle of events in life such as seed-time and harvest. The stress laid on the actual ability of the worshipper himself and upon his dependence on the power with which he is concerned may also vary significantly. In short, no hastily generalised meaning should be ascribed to actions of this kind, even though a widespread form of action itself can be discerned.

1.4.1 The five great sacrifices

Five are the great sacrifices; they are the great continuous sacrifices : the propitiation of all things created, of human beings, of the forefathers, of the gods, and of the sacred lore. Everyone should make offerings to all creatures; thereby one achieves the propitiation of all creatures. Every day one should make gifts, even if it be only with a cup of water : thus one achieves the propitiation of human beings. Every day one should, even if it be only with a cup of water, make offerings to his ancestors : thus one achieves the propitiation of the forefathers. Every day one should make offerings to the gods, even if it be only with sacred twigs (and fire) : thus one achieves propitiation of the gods. Then, the propitiation of the sacred lore : learning of one's own Veda is that propitiation. Speech, mind, and intellect are the various utensils of this sacrifice. Truth is the final purificatory ceremony; heaven is the end. He who understands this and every day does his sacred study, gains three times the world that is gained by one who fills the whole world with wealth and gives it away. Hence, one should study his own sacred scriptures. Morgan (ed). *The Religion of the Hindus* (New York 1953), 292-3 (*Śukla Yajurveda, Śatapatha Brāhmaṇa* XI, 3)

1.4.2 Threefold worship

Vedic, Tāntric, and mixed, threefold is my worship. One may follow his wishes in choosing any of the forms. A twice-born may worship me, his Lord, through devotion, with materials, in an image, on the raised ground, on fire, in the sun, in water, or in his heart. After finishing the morning prayer sanctioned by the Veda he is to offer worship with his mind firmly fixed. Mobile or immobile, both types of images serve as his shrine or my abode by installation, with this difference, that there is no invocation and no sending away in immobile ones. The sincere devotee worships me with well-arranged offerings on images in case he has a fancy for the fruits of worship. If he has no such, he may perform with the things he can procure.

For him who worships in the heart, his attitude of reverence is what matters. The daily bath and ornaments I like in case I am worshipped in images, the placing of the deity and his accessories in proper parts of the body is what pleases me if worship be on the raised ground . . . Morgan, *The Religion of the Hindus,* 193-4 *(Bhāgavata Purāṇa* XI. 27)

1.4.3 Sacrifice for sin atonement

If any one of the common people sins unwittingly in doing any one of the things which the Lord has commanded not to be done, and is guilty, when the sin which he has committed is made known to him he shall bring for his offering a goat, a female without blemish, for his sin which he has committed. And he shall lay his hand on the head of the sin offering, and kill the sin offering in the place of burnt offering. And the priest shall take some of its blood with his finger and put it on the horns of the altar of burnt offering, and pour out the rest of its blood at the base of the altar. And all its fat he shall remove, as the fat is removed from the peace offerings, and the priest shall burn it upon the altar for a pleasing odour to the Lord; and the priest shall make atonement for him, and he shall be forgiven. Leviticus iv, 27-31

1.4.4 Songs of praise

O come, let us sing to the Lord; let us make a joyful noise to the rock of our salvation!

D

Let us come into his presence with thanksgiving; let us make a joyful noise to him with songs of praise!

For the Lord is a great God, and a great King above all gods.

In his hand are the depths of the earth; the heights of the mountains are his also.

The sea is his, for he made it; for his hands formed the dry land.

O come, let us worship and bow down, let us kneel before the Lord, our Maker!

For he is our God, and we are the people of his pasture, and the sheep of his hand. Psalms xcv. 1-7

1.4.5 The sacrifice of the mass

Be pleased, O God, to bless this offering, to give it your full approval, to make it perfect and worthy of your acceptance, so that it may become for us the Body and Blood of your beloved Son, our Lord Jesus Christ.

The consecration

The day before he suffered, he took bread into his holy, worshipful hands, and with eyes lifted up to heaven, to you God, his almighty Father, giving thanks to you, he blessed, broke and gave it to his disciples, saying: Take and eat you all of this,

FOR THIS IS MY BODY.

So too, when the meal was over, he took this noble cup in his holy, worshipful hands, and, again giving thanks to you, he blessed it and gave it to his disciples, saying: Take it, all of you, and drink,

FOR THE FORGIVENESS OF SINS.
OF THE NEW AND ETERNAL COVENANT
—THE MYSTERY OF FAITH—
WHICH SHALL BE SHED FOR YOU
AND FOR THE MANY
FOR THIS IS THE CUP OF MY BLOOD,

As often as you do these things, you shall do them in memory of me.

Prayers of offering.

We do indeed, Lord, remember the blessed Passion of the same Christ your Son, our Lord, his resurrection from the dead and his ascension to glory in heaven, and we, your servants, with your holy people offer to your resplendent majesty, from the gifts which you yourself have given to us, the perfect sacrifice, the holy sacrifice, the unblemished sacrifice, the holy bread of eternal life, and the Cup of everlasting salvation.

The sacrifices of the Old Testament were accepted by God; Christ's sacrifice is even more acceptable.

Look on these offerings with favour and contentment. Accept them as you graciously accepted the offerings of your just servant Abel, the sacrifice of our father Abraham, and that of your high priest Melchisedech—a holy sacrifice, an unblemished victim.

We humbly beseech you, almighty God, to command that these offerings be carried by your holy Angel to your altar in heaven, in the sight of your divine majesty. May we, who receive your Son's most sacred Body and Blood at this altar here, be filled with every heavenly blessing and grace; through the same Christ our Lord. Amen. *Peoples Mass Book* (London, Dublin and Melbourne 1966), 24-6.

This extract indicates the words only, not the complete action.

1.4.6 Self-immolation

Immediately after . . . the Bodhisattva . . . in presence of those eighty-four thousand Stûpas, burnt his own arm which was marked by the one hundred auspicious signs, and so paid worship to those Stûpas containing the relics of the Tathâgata, during seventy-two thousand years.

Now . . . the young man or young lady of good family striving in the Bodhisattva vehicle towards the goal and longing for supreme, perfect enlightenment, who at the Tathâgata-shrines shall burn a great toe, a finger, a toe, or a whole limb . . . shall produce far more pious merit, far more than results from giving up a kingdom, sons, daughters, and wives . . . H. Kern (trans). *Saddharma-Puṇḍarīka or The Lotus of the True Law*. Max Müller (ed). Sacred Books of the East, XXI (1884, New York 1963), 385-6

A Bodhisattva is a future Buddha (Tathâgata) and the Bodhisattva vehicle is the Mahayana path towards Buddhahood as opposed to that of other Buddhist schools

---

1.5 REHEARSAL OF SIGNIFICANT PAST OR MYTH

One extensive example of this type of religious action has already been given in the extract from the Roman Catholic Mass (1.4.5), and three more cases follow below. The extent to which the events rehearsed 'really' happened or not, or the sense in which they are believed to have done so, are questions which might be answered differently in different cases. Indeed the category might be extended to include the rehearsal of 'pure' myth, such as the creation myth used at the Babylonian new year festival (cf the summary account in S. H. Hooke's *Middle Eastern Mythology* (Harmondsworth 1963), 41-6), but not all myths are rehearsed liturgically.

1.5.1 Recital of the Haggadah

At this stage, it is customary to remove the egg and the bone and to uncover the Mazzoth upon which attention is thereby concentrated. The tray is then lifted up and displayed to the company, of whom those who are nearest put out their hands to assist in supporting it, while the Celebrant recites the following formula :

This is the bread of affliction that our fathers ate in the land of Egypt. All who are hungered—let them come and eat : all who are needy—let them come and celebrate the Passover. Now we

are here, but next year may we be in the land of Israel! Now we
are slaves, but next year may we be free men!

The tray is put down, the Mazzoth covered, and the other objects replaced upon it. The second cup of wine is then filled, and
the youngest present asks the Four Questions:

Wherein is this night different from all other nights? For, on
all other nights, we may eat either leavened bread or unleavened,
but on this night only unleavened: on all other nights we may eat
other kinds of herb, but on this night only bitter herbs: on all
other nights we need not dip our herbs even once, but on this
night we do so twice: on all other nights we eat either sitting upright or reclining, but on this night we all recline.

The Mazzoth are uncovered, and the Celebrant replies:

'We were Pharaoh's bondmen in Egypt: and the Lord our
God brought us out therefrom with a mighty hand' (Deut. vi. 21)
and an outstretched arm. Now, if the Holy One, blessed be He,
had not brought our fathers forth from Egypt, then we, and our
children, and our children's children, would be servants to
Pharaoh in Egypt. Therefore, even were we all wise, all men of
understanding, all advanced in years, and all endowed with
knowledge of the Torah, it would nevertheless be our duty to tell
the story of the coming forth from Egypt: and the more a man
tells of the coming forth from Egypt, the more is he to be praised.
Cecil Roth (ed and trans). *The Haggadah* (1959), 9-12
Mazzoth are unleavened bread.

1.5.2 The stations of the cross

Among the many Christian pilgrims to the Holy Land there were
some who, not content with the happiness of visiting in person
the places made dear by the sufferings of our Blessed Lord, trans-
ferred, if I may so speak, Mount Calvary to their own homes. In
order that they might, in spirit, often revisit these memorable
places, they erected in quiet groves, or upon the side of a hill, a
number of crosses in imitation of the spots on Mount Calvary
venerated for some incident in the Passion of our Lord. They
then visited successively the places marked by the crosses, stopping

for a short time to meditate upon the sufferings of the Redeemer. To aid their imagination, and the better to fix their minds upon the subject of their contemplation, they frequently attached to these crosses pictures or paintings representing some scene in the Passion. This devotion was called *'The Way of the Cross'*, and the pictures or representations were termed 'Stations'.

The number of the stations . . . is fourteen . . .

1. Jesus is condemned to death by Pilate.
2. Jesus is laden with the cross.
3. Jesus falls under the weight of the cross.
4. Jesus meets his Mother.
5. Simon of Cyrene helps Jesus to carry the cross.
6. Veronica offers Jesus her head-cloth.
7. Jesus falls a second time under the cross.
8. Jesus comforts the women of Jerusalem.
9. Jesus falls a third time under the cross.
10. Jesus is stripped of his garments.
11. Jesus is nailed to the cross.
12. Jesus dies upon the cross.
13. Jesus is taken down from the cross.
14. Jesus is laid in the tomb.

F. J. Shadler (trans). *The Beauties of the Catholic Church; or, Her Festivals, and Her Rites and Ceremonies, Popularly Explained* (New York 1881), 136-7

1.5.3 What happened in the Māgha month

Today is the Full Moon Day of the Third Lunar Month on which Our Lord Buddha, the Exalted One, the Fully Enlightened One, delivered the discourse on the main principles of His teachings which are called 'Ovādapātimokkhā', to the great assembly of Bikkhus at the Veluvana Vihāra. This was a wonderful event because four unique things happened :—

1. The Noble Disciples, 1250 in number came to this meeting without any previous announcement.
2. All of them were ordained by the Lord Buddha Himself.
3. All of them were Liberated (Arahant.)

4. It was the Full Moon Day of the Māgha Month.

Then the Blessed One delivered the discourse on the Purification known as the Visuddhi-Uposatha.

The day of that Great Assembly, is celebrated annually. We Buddhists recall, that the Buddha Our Supreme Master passed away long ago, entering into Nirvāna, which is Extinction without Remainder. We have come to pay our sincere homage to Him together with His Holy Order, 1250 in number, we pay respect and are aware of the fact that the awakening is in us, that we have Buddha-Nature. We do this by offering these flowers, the incense and candles to the image representing the Buddha.

May the Great Merit that comes about by these offerings protect us, and guard us. May it bring us blessing and happiness for ever and ever.

May all beings be well, may all beings be happy-minded and live in peace. Ven. Phra Mahā Vichitr Tissidatto. *Buddhist Holy Days* (1966), 10

The Venerable Tissidatto has translated this from a Pali text used in Thailand.

1.6 MEDITATION AND PRAYER

'Meditation' and 'prayer' are closely associated with the rehearsal of myth or of the significant past (1.5) and with religious action seeking specific benefits (1.7). If we disregard at this point the varied conceptual intentions of the practitioners, a wide spectrum of comparably routinised devotions may be discerned. These range between systematic recitation of specified texts, the repetition of actual 'prayers', guided thinking on specified topics drawn from the belief system, and more or less organised silence (which is very difficult to quote from). Cf 5.2.

1.6.1 Meditation in brief and in detail

Suppose two bhikkus are reciting a text with many elided

repetitions, then the bhikkhu with the quicker understanding fills out the elided repetitions once or twice, after which he goes on doing the recital with only the two end parts of the elisions. Here the one of less quick understanding says 'What is he reciting? Why, he does not even give one time to move one's lips! If the recitation is done like this, when shall we ever get familiar with the text!', and so he does his recitation filling out each elision as it comes. Then the other says, 'What is he reciting? Why, he never lets one get to the end of it! If the recitation is done like this, when shall we ever get to the end of it!' So too, the detailed discerning of the elements by head hairs, etc., appears redundant to one of quick understanding, though the meditation subject becomes clear to him if he gives his attention to it in brief in this way 'What has the characteristic of stiffenedness is the earth element', and so on. But when the other gives his attention to it in this way, it appears obscure and unevident, and it only becomes plain to him if he gives his attention in detail by head hairs and so on. Bhikkhu Ñyāṇamoli (trans). *The Path of Purification* (Visuddhi-Magga) by Bhadantacariya Buddhaghosa (Colombo 1964), 384-5

The meditation in detail involves, in this case, going through the constituent parts of the body one by one, thus: head hairs, body hairs, nails, teeth, skin, flesh, sinews, bones, bone marrow, kidney, heart, liver, etc, leading ultimately to the abolition of the perception of living beings.

1.6.2 The Ignatian method

Prayer is the lifting up of the whole soul, the whole being to God—imagination, intellect, affections and will. In the earlier stages of the prayer life this has to be done explicitly and deliberately, and it is the purpose of this method to do this . . .

SCHEME OF THE IGNATION METHOD

(1) *The Preparation*
   Remote.

Mortification.
Recollection.
Humility.
Proximate.
Consideration of the subject.
Recalling the subject.
Consecration.
Immediate.
Recollection of the Presence of God.
Act of Humility.
Prayer to the Holy Ghost.
(2) *The Exercise*.
  i. Composition of Place.
  ii. Petition.
  (a) Recollection. (The Memory.)
  (b) Considerations. (The Intellect.)
  (c) Colloquies. (The Will [affective].)
  (d) Resolution. (The Will [conative].)
(3) *The Conclusion*.
Gathering up the fruits of the meditation.

F. P. Harton. *The Elements of the Spiritual Life : A Study in Ascetical Theology* (1932), 233 and 239

This method was first articulated by Ignatius Loyola in a work entitled *The Spiritual Exercises* (1541).

1.6.3 Indulgenced prayers

I. PRAYER BEFORE A CRUCIFIX

Behold, O most kind and sweet Jesus, I cast myself on my knees in Thy sight, and with the most fervent desire of my soul, I pray and beseech Thee that Thou wouldst impress upon my heart lively sentiments of faith, hope and charity, with true repentance for my sins, and a firm desire for amendment, while with deep affection and grief of soul I ponder within myself and mentally contemplate Thy five most precious wounds; having before my eyes that which David spake in prophecy of Thee,

O good Jesus : 'They pierced My hands and My feet; they have numbered all My bones.'

Indulgence of 10 years.

Plenary indulgence on the usual conditions, if said looking at a crucifix.

Pius IX. July 31, 1858 . . .

XI. DAILY PRAYERS AND INVOCATIONS

. . . Eternal Father, I offer Thee the Most Precious Blood of Jesus Christ in atonement for my sins, and in supplication for the holy souls in purgatory and for the needs of the holy Church. *500 days.*

My Jesus, mercy. *300 days.*

Sweetest Jesus, be not to me a Judge, but a Saviour. *300 days . . .*

JESUS. *For invoking devoutly the Holy Name* : *300 days.*

W. Raemers (C.SS.R). *Indulgenced Prayers* (Catholic Truth Society, 1956), 11, 16, 20-1

An indulgence is believed to remit all or part of the temporal punishment due to sin which would otherwise have to be undergone on earth or in purgatory.

1.6.4 Memorisation of the Koran

O Allah! Originator of the heavens and the earth,
Lord of majesty, glory,
And of might incomprehensible!
I beseech Thee, O Allah,
O Beneficent Lord,
In the name of Thy Majesty and
Of the Light of Thy Countenance,
To cause my heart to retain
Thy Scripture even as Thou has taught [it unto me].
And grant that I may recite it
In such a manner as will cause
Thee to be well pleased with me.
O Allah! Originator of the heavens and the earth,
Lord of majesty, glory,

And of might incomprehensible!
I beseech Thee, O Beneficent Lord!
In the name of Thy Majesty,
And of the Light of Thy Countenance,
To illuminate my sight with Thy Scripture,
To set free my tongue,
To comfort my heart therewith,
And to wash my body therewith.
For indeed! none helps me
In [the path of] truth besides Thee
And favours me besides Thee.
There is no strength nor power
Save in Allah, the Exalted, the Magnificent.

M. Abdul Hamid Siddiqi. *Prayers of the Prophet* (*Masnūn Du'ā'ain*) (Lahore 1968), 32-3

This prayer is to be said in the third part of Friday night before reciting selected sūrahs of the Koran.

1.7 SEEKING SPECIFIC BENEFITS

Almost every religious tradition offers forms of action to be undertaken with a view to securing specific benefits. The variety of such benefits is as great as the variety of human needs and desires, but perhaps the most frequent benefits sought are those connected with the growth of food (hence the importance of rain), economic prosperity, success in battle, defence against natural disasters such as epidemic and flood, healing of disease, and exorcism of malevolent spirits. Matters which cannot be pursued here are the relationships between magic, religion and science. Suffice it to say that one should beware of imputing oversimplified or alien notions of cause and effect, particularly in the case of seasonal rituals such as those of rogationtide and harvest. Conversely, a modern notion of cause and effect is not necessarily accompanied by the abandonment of ritual.

1.7.1 Prayer for various benefits (i)

Among the Brāhmans, may the Brāhman be born with spiritual lustre; in this country, may the king be born a warrior, a capable archer and chariot-fighter; may the cow be born a milch cow; the ox a good draught ox; the horse a fleet one; the damsel the object of the city's admiration; the fighter victorious; and the youth fit for the assembly; may a hero be born to the performer of the sacrifice; whenever we wish may the cloud rain; may our vegetation ripen with fruits; may there be for us acquisition and conserving [of prosperity]. Morgan. *The Religion of the Hindus*, 294 (*Kṛishṇa Yajurveda* VII. 5. 18. 1)

According to Morgan this prayer is a favourite with many Indian writers and public figures, who would like to see it in use as a national prayer.

1.7.2 Prayer for various benefits (ii)

When heaven is shut up and there is no rain because they have sinned against thee, if they pray toward this place [the temple built by Solomon], and acknowledge thy name, and turn from their sin, when thou dost afflict them, then hear thou in heaven, and forgive the sin of thy servants, thy people Israel, when thou dost teach them the good way in which they should walk; and grant rain upon thy land, which thou hast given to thy people as an inheritance.

If there is famine in the land, if there is pestilence or blight or mildew or locust or caterpillar; if their enemy besieges them in any of their cities; whatever plague, whatever sickness there is; . . . then hear thou in heaven thy dwelling place, and forgive, and act . . . 1 Kings, viii, 35-7, 39

1.7.3 A cure for potato degeneration

Chairman Mao said . . . 'The intellectuals will accomplish nothing if they fail to integrate themselves with the workers and peasants.'

The teachings of our great leader Chairman Mao lit up the

way ahead for the revolutionary science workers, and corrected
the course of this research programme. Stepping out of their
laboratories, they successively went to the countryside . . . and
collected a lot of experience in preventing potato degeneration
accumulated by the masses of peasants during their practice of
production over a long period of time.

When the revolutionary scientists, raising high the great red
banner of Mao Tse-tung's thought, carried on this work, the
handful of Party persons in authority taking the capitalist road
viciously sneered, 'What experience could you sum up from the
masses but the same old peasant stuff?' . . . After some successes
were achieved in this work, the reactionary bourgeois academic
'authorities' again mocked, 'It's neither science nor theory', in
a vain attempt to negate them. But all this did not cow the
revolutionary science workers armed with the invincible thought
of Mao Tse-tung . . .

'Sailing the seas depends on the helmsman; making revolution
depends on Mao Tse-tung's thought.' Revolutionary science
workers of the Institute of Genetics persist in creatively studying
and applying Chairman Mao's writings while working in the
countryside.

Commune members in Chiehshou County, Anhwei Province,
grew the local variety of potato and reaped bumper harvests.
This is a great victory for the invincible thought of Mao Tse-
tung. *China Pictorial* (Peking 1968, September), 38-40 (text
and picture captions).

Illustrations depict group study of Mao's writings, slogans, flags
and portraits of Mao, set amidst the potato fields and specimens
of the harvest.

1.7.4 Prayers for rain (i)

25th day. The Ministers conversed with one another, saying:
'In accordance with the teachings of the village hafuri, there
have been in some places horses and cattle killed as a sacrifice
to the Gods of the various (Shintō) shrines, in others frequent

changes of the market-places, or prayers to the River-Gods. None of these practices have had hitherto any good result.' Then Soga no Oho-omi answered and said 'The "Mahāyāna Sutra" ought to be read by way of extract in the temples, our sins repented of, as Buddha teaches, and thus with humility rain should be prayed for.'

27th day. In the South Court of the Great Temple, the images of Buddha and of the Bosatsu, and the images of the four Heavenly Kings, were magnificently adorned. A multitude of priests, by humble request, read the 'Mahāyāna Sutra.' On this occasion Soga no Oho-omi held a censer in his hands, and having burnt incense in it, put up a prayer.

28th day. A slight rain fell.

29th day. The prayers for rain being unsuccessful, the reading of the 'Sutra' was discontinued.

8th month, 1st day. The Emperor made a progress to the river-source of Minabuchi. Here he knelt down and prayed, worshipping towards the four quarters and looking up to Heaven. Straightway there was thunder and a great rain, which eventually fell for five days, and plentifully bedewed the Empire.
Aston. *Nihongi* Part Two, 174-5

The village *hafuri* was the priest of the local shrine. In looking up to 'Heaven' (*ten* or *t'ien*) the Emperor was following Chinese (non-Buddhist) practice. On other occasions Buddhist priests were more successful.

1.7.5 Prayers for rain (ii)

At the time of drought
O Allah! give us the drink;
O Allah! bless us with rainfall . .

At the time of rainfall
O Allah! make it a profitable downpour.

When there is an excessive downpour

O Allah! let there be downpour in our suburbs,
But not on us.
Let the rain fall on hillocks,
In the thickets, on the mountains,
Rivers, and on the hotbeds of plantations.

Siddiqi, *Prayers of the Prophet* (Masnūn Du'ā'ain), 41-2

1.7.6 Prayers for rain (iii)

For rain. O GOD, heavenly Father, who by thy Son Jesus
Christ hast promised to all them that seek thy kingdom, and the
righteousness thereof, all things necessary to their bodily susten-
ance; Send us, we beseech thee, in this our necessity, such mod-
erate rain and showers, that we may receive the fruits of the
earth to our comfort and to thy honour; through Jesus Christ
our Lord. Amen. *Book of Common Prayer,* from the section
entitled 'Prayers and Thanksgivings upon Several Occasions'

Cf also in the same source the immediately following prayer 'for
fair weather'.

1.8 OCCASIONAL RITES

A very large number of religious rituals or ceremonies are related to special occasions of individual life which are repeated
more or less regularly, as required, in the life of the community. Some are seasonal and occupational, being connected
with seedtime and harvest, hunting, fishing, building, etc.
Others are to do with birth (below), adolescence (cf 5.3),
marriage and death (cf 2.2.1 and 6.5). For a famous detailed
discussion of such rites in their social and psychological context see Van Gennep's *The Rites of Passage* (1908, Chicago
1960).

1.8.1 Disposal of an umbilical cord

The baby is washed, and then the mother; and there are spells for both of these performances too The umbilical cord and afterbirth are wrapped in white muslin, put into a jug, salted, and buried outside the house, in front if the child is a boy, in back if it is a girl, although some people bury both in front, the boy to the left of the door, the girl to the right. A little wicker fence is erected around the spot or a broken earthenware pot is inverted over it to keep dogs or other animals from digging it up, and a small candle is kept burning over it for thirty-five days in order to prevent evil spirits from disturbing it.

> In the name of God, the Merciful, the Compassionate!
> Father Earth, Mother Earth,
> I am about to leave in your care the birthcord of the baby.
> Thus the baby itself I leave behind [i.e., I don't bury it],
> Only the umbilical cord do I leave in your care.
> Don't bother the baby,
> This is necessary because of Allah.
> If you do bother him, you will be punished by God.
> Cast away the childhood illnesses from the baby,
> This too is necessary because of Allah.
> Birthcord, thus I leave you in someone else's care.
> Little baby, don't oppose your father,
> Or you will be punished by Allah.

The burying of the umbilical cord is a serious matter. One woman blamed the death of her child, in convulsion after forty days of life, on the fact that the midwife did not put enough salt in the umbilical cord when she buried it, and so it 'came up' and the child died. The cord and afterbirth, coming as it does after the birth of the child, is considered to be his spirit younger brother, while the amniotic fluid which precedes him (it is thrown out up into the air) is considered to be his spirit older brother. For the first thirty-five days they remain near the child and protect him against illness, the first under the ground, the other in the sky. Clifford Geertz. *The Religion of Java* (New York 1960), 46

1.8.2 Laws of circumcision

It is a positive precept for a father to circumcise his son or to appoint another Israelite to act as his agent who knows the Laws of circumcision, and is careful and zealous in the performance of this precept and qualified for performing the act of circumcision. If the father be incompetent to circumcise, and if the operator in attendance refuse to circumcise gratuitously, but only for remuneration, such a person should be censured by the ecclesiastical authorities. The father should place his son upon the knees of the God-father and hand the knife to the operator and stand near him during the circumcision to indicate that the former is his agent.

The circumcision shall not be performed until sunrise of the eighth day after his birth, that entire day being the proper time for its performance, but the zealous hasten to fulfil the precepts, wherefore the circumcision is to be performed forthwith in the morning. The circumcision, which (for certain reasons) is not performed at the appointed time (on the eighth day), can only be performed in the daytime. Gerald Friedlander (trans). *Laws and Customs of Israel, Compiled from the Codes Chayye Adam ('Life of Man') Kizzur Shulchan Aruch ('Condensed Code of Laws')* (1924), 183-4

Circumcision is a widespread birth rite among Semetic and other peoples.

1.8.3 Service at a circumcision

Upon the arrival of the Child who is to be initiated into the Covenant of Abraham, those present at the Ceremony rise and say:
Blessed be he that cometh.

The Father of the Child says:

I am here ready to perform the affirmative precept to circumcise my son, even as the Creator, blessed be he, hath commanded us, as it is written in the Law. And he that is eight days

E

old shall be circumcised among you, every male throughout your generations.

The Mohel takes the Child, and, placing it upon a seat, says:
This is the throne of Elijah : may he be remembered for good!
For thy salvation I have waited, O Lord. I have hoped, O Lord, for thy salvation; and have done thy commandments. I have hoped for thy salvation, O Lord. I rejoice at thy word, as one that findeth great spoil. Great peace have they who love thy Law; and there is no stumbling for them. Happy is he whom thou choosest, and causest to approach that he may dwell in thy courts.

Those present respond:

O let us be satisfied with the goodness of thy house, thy holy temple.

The Mohel places the Child upon the knees of the Sandek, and before performing the Circumcision says the following Blessing:
Blessed art thou, O Lord our God, King of the universe, who hast sanctified us by thy commandments, and hast commanded us concerning the Circumcision.

Immediately after the Circumcision the Father says the following Blessing:
Blessed art thou, O Lord our God, King of the universe, who hast sanctified us by thy commandments, and hast commanded us to make our sons enter into the covenant of Abraham our father.

Those present respond:
Even as this child has entered into the covenant, so may he enter into the Law, the nuptial canopy, and into good deeds.
Israel Brodie (ed). *The Authorised Daily Prayer Book of the United Hebrew Congregations of the British Commonwealth of Nations* (1962), 401-2

1.9 ETHICS AND SOCIETY

Religious action takes place not only in a special sphere of its own, but is also worked out in a variety of ways in the world at large. The following extracts show religion believed to be intrinsically connected with correct social relations; the clear-cut determination of roles expected to be played in society; more individually orientated and thereby universal ethical pronouncements; and religion as the mainspring of political action. In all such cases the civic or legal, social, individual ethical, or political act remains at the same time a religious act.

1.9.1 Rites and reliability

When those at the top love the rites, the people will of necessity be respectful; when justice is observed at the top, the people will be submissive; when reliability reigns at the top, the people will be sincere. Ware. *The Sayings of Confucius,* 83 (XIII, 4)

1.9.2 Muslim law

The members of the Commission are of the firm conviction that the principles of law and specific injunctions of the Holy *Qur'an,* if rationally and liberally interpreted, are capable of establishing absolute justice between human beings and are conducive to healthy and happy family life . . . We have to go back to the original spirit of the *Qur'an* and the *Sunnah* and lay special emphasis on those trends in basic Islam that are conducive to healthy adaptations to our present circumstances . . .

The Commission considers the four sources of Muslim law enunciated by the great *Imams* as comprehensive: The Holy *Qur'an, Sunnah, Ijma* (Consensus) and *Qiyas* (Reasoning by analogy), and intends to make proposals in accordance with one or the other. Khurshid Ahmad (ed). *Studies in the Family Law of Islam* (Karachi 1961), 46

The passage is from the report of a Commission on Marriage

and Family Law, whose approach is hotly debated in the volume as a whole. The Commission also emphasises the importance of the principles of *Istihsan* ('common weal') and *Ijtihad* ('exertion to form an independent judgement'), which taken together make Muslim law infinitely flexible. *Sunnah,* above, means tradition concerning the words and deeds of the prophet.

1.9.3 The housewife (i)

The housewife should always be joyous, adept at domestic work, neat in her domestic wares, and restrained in expenses. The woman has no independent sacrific to perform, no vow, no fasting; by serving her husband, she is honoured in the heavens. On the death of her husband, the chaste wife, established in continence, reaches heaven, even if childless, like students who have practiced self-control. Morgan. *The Religion of the Hindus,* 330 (*Laws of Manu* V)

1.9.4 The housewife (ii)

Parents would do well, *early* to instil into the minds of their daughters this view of female duty; lest in training them to shine in the *world,* by a display of worldly advantages, they neglect to train them for the exercise of Christian graces—self-denial, meekness and humility—in the less dazzling, though more important sphere of *home.* John James (Prebendary of Peterborough), *A Comment upon the Collects* (1877), 318, n2

1.9.5 Buddhist ethics

Five branches of moral training, to wit, abhorrence of murder, theft, inchastity, lying, and intemperance in drink. T. W. and C. A. F. Rhys Davids (trans). *Dialogues of the Buddha Part III* (1921, 1965), 225 (*Sangiti Suttanta* V, ix)

These are the basic points of Buddhist lay morals, mere preliminaries to the monastic path.

1.9.6 Love your enemies

'You have learned that they were told, "Love your neighbour, hate your enemy." But what I tell you is this: Love your enemies and pray for your persecutors; only so can you be children of your heavenly Father, who makes his sun rise on good and bad alike, and sends the rain on the honest and the dishonest.' Matthew v, 43-5

1.9.7 Conquest by the holy people

When the Lord your God brings you into the land which you are entering to take possession of it, and clears away many nations before you, the Hittites [etc], and when the Lord your God gives them over to you, and you defeat them; then you must utterly destroy them; you shall make no covenant with them, and show no mercy to them. You shall not make marriages with them, giving your daughters to their sons or taking their daughters for your sons. For they would turn away your sons from following me, to serve other gods; then the anger of the Lord would be kindled against you, and he would destroy you quickly. But thus shall you deal with them : you shall break down their altars, and dash in pieces their pillars, and hew down their Asherim, and burn their graven images with fire. For you are a people holy to the Lord your God; the Lord your God has chosen you to be a people for his own possession, out of all the peoples that are on the face of the earth. Deuteronomy vii, 1-6

'Asherim' were wooden poles of cultic importance in Canaanite religion.

1.9.8 Kingdom of heaven on earth

We have been led step by step to a profound realisation of a love which unites us in a spiritual fellowship with seekers everywhere.

We have tried to face very frankly the facts of the world as it is, knowing that this must be our point of departure for the world as it ought to be. The war has aroused us to a sense of the moral failure of a civilisation which thwarts the practice of love in our social and international relationships. We have faith that out of the chaos of today will emerge a new order. This will be achieved as we individually strive to live so that the Divine Spirit is liberated in us ...

With the humility born of our failure to live out the principles we profess, yet with the boldness of those who feel the greatness of their message, we would throw in our lives with all men and women who are sharing in the adventure of establishing the Kingdom of Heaven on Earth. Yearly Meeting, 1921. *Christian Life Faith and Thought in the Society of Friends* (1922), 122-3 (Minute of the International Conference of Young Friends).

1.10 PROPAGATION

The self-conscious attempt to propagate beliefs and practices, as opposed to the mere handing down of them to posterity, is a good example of a type of religious action which is clearly 'religious' but yet not common to all religions. Two quotations from Buddhist sources follow, because Buddhists sometimes claim that they do not attempt to 'convert' others to Buddhism; and one other example is adduced for balance.

1.10.1 The Buddha's words to Māra

I shall not die, O Evil One! until the brethren and sisters of the Order, and until the lay-disciples of either sex shall have become true hearers, wise and well trained, ready and learned, carrying the doctrinal books in their memory, masters of the lesser corollaries that follow from the larger doctrine, correct in life, walking according to the precepts—until they, having thus themselves learned the doctrine, shall be able to tell others of it, preach it, make it known, establish it, open it, minutely explain it and make it clear—until they, when others start vain doctrine easy to be refuted by the truth, shall be able in refuting it, to spread the wonder-working truth abroad! Rhys Davids, *Dialogues of the Buddha Part II*, 112 (*Mahâ Parinibbâna Suttanta III* 7)

1.10.2 Converting the ignorant

The Fifth Patriarch instructed me : 'Leave, work hard, take the Dharma with you to the south. For three years do not spread the teaching or else calamity will befall the Dharma. Later work to convert people; you must guide deluded persons well. If you are able to awaken another's mind, he will be no different from me.' . . .

> If you wish to convert an ignorant person,
> Then you must have expedients.
> Do not allow him to have doubts,
> Then enlightenment (*bodhi*) will appear.

Philip B. Yampolsky (trans). *The Platform Sutra of the Sixth Patriarch* (New York 1967), 133 and 161.

This 'sutra' is one of the classic texts of Ch'an (Zen) Buddhism 'Expedients' are forms of teaching which are not themselves the real truth but which are conducive to a recognition of the latter.

1.10.3 The conversion of Latin America

As far as your above-said envoys could judge, these peoples inhabiting the said islands and lands believe that one God-Creator is in Heaven; they seem to be well fitted to embrace the Catholic faith and to be imbued with good morals; and there is hope that, were they instructed, the name of the Saviour, our Lord Jesus Christ, could be easily introduced into these lands and islands . . .

And in some islands and lands which have already been discovered gold, spices and very many precious things of various categories and qualities have been found.

Wherefore, all things considered maturely and, as it becomes Catholic kings and princes, considered with special regard for

the exaltation and spread of the Catholic faith—as your forefathers, kings of illustrious memory, used to do—you have decided to subdue the said mainlands and islands, and their natives
and inhabitants, with God's grace, and to bring them to the
Catholic faith. Anne Fremantle. *The Papal Encyclicals in their
Historical Context* (New York 1956), 78 (from Alexander VI's
papal bull *Inter Ceterae Divinae* 1493)

The bull goes on to grant jurisdiction to Spain over any lands discovered west of a line running from pole to pole, one hundred
leagues west of the Azores and Cape Verde Islands. Although the
history of Christian missions is very complex, the religious motivation to spread the faith should not be under-estimated.

PART TWO

Religious Groups

At a later stage (section 6 below) some mention will be made of the relationships between religion and other social factors, but for the moment we are concerned with a simple question only. Who is supposed to be involved in a given example of religion? Working on the fundamental observation that, in a given human society, those involved in a selected example of religion will either be everybody or they will be not-everybody, there seem to be four main possible answers to the question.

If everybody is involved, at least supposedly, it may be asked whether they are also involved in further cases of religion other than that under consideration. If they are not, as may well seem to be the case in relatively small, homogeneous societies, then we may speak of 'simple group religion' as in 2.1 below. If the society is more complex, however, and contains various forms of association within itself, some of them perhaps being religious groups in their own right, then it seems appropriate to call the religion of the whole society 'civil religion' as in 2.2 below. One of the characteristics of civil religion is that many of those supposedly involved may be weak in interest and lax in performance, their stronger personal attachments being to some other group or groups, religious or otherwise.

In cases of religion where some members only of an otherwise coherent society are involved, it may be asked whether their involvement is miscellaneous and incidental, or whether they form a recognisable and coherent subgroup of which they themselves are aware. If the involvement is miscellaneous and incidental, as for example when some people in Britain may be found to share belief in, say, the workings of fate, and to share the practice of not walking under ladders or on the lines between paving stones, then it is appropriate to speak of 'folk religion' as in 2.3 below. If however there is a coherent group in evidence such as might be called a 'sect', a 'cult', a 'community' or a denomination', then it is appropriate to speak of a 'minor group religion' as in 2.4 below.

Finally it is also possible to consider various types of religious 'specialist' : priests, kings, prophets, teachers, ascetics, and so on (2.5 below), who perform various specialised roles in the various religious groups categorised above. This is a slightly different category, therefore, being one of social differentiation within given religious groups, and its subdivisions may be related to any of the above four main groups. Further subdivision of this category runs into problems similar to those encountered in the characterisation of religious action (cf above, 37f).

The four main categories have perforce been very simply separated from each other above, and this may suggest that individual cases can be dropped neatly into one or other of them. This would be far from the truth, unless indeed we were to consider religions as they exist only at separate isolated points of time. The reality of religion is constant change, however slow. This means that what one day may come into existence as a minor group religion may later become established as a civil religion, and later still it may decay, only for elements of it to persist here and there without coherent social grouping as folk religion. Another possibility is that a simple group religion may persist through various historical changes and gradually become the civil religion of a very complex society. The movement from simple *ujigami* religions (cf 2.1.1 and 5.6.2) to the Shinto-Confucian civil religion of nineteenth-century Japan (cf 2.2.3) is an example of this. Such complications really lead to questions which can only be answered by means of a more complex comparative approach (cf 5.3, 5.6, 5.7, 6.4 and 6.5).

It should be clearly understood that these four categories are by no means intended to offer a functional theory of religion in society, and such a theory might well cut across the divisions given at this point. For example, simple group religion and civil religion might be said to perform exactly the same integrative function in society, while minor group religion might be thought to perform variously integrative or revitalising functions. These lines of thought are explanatory in purpose and fall in principle into section 6 below. All that is said here does not go beyond the phenomenological approach to the actions and beliefs of the participants themselves; that is to say that although the categorisation is of course an abstract one, it does not in principle question or subvert the possible truth of the beliefs held by the participants.

The intention at this point is simply to indicate the general comparability of the social shapes of religion, because this is what is required at this point in the organisation of religious data. This limitation should be noted or false conclusions may be drawn.

2.1 SIMPLE GROUP RELIGION

Simple group religion is coterminous with a small group of persons associated as a family or clan, or else by geography and livelihood. Thus it may involve household, ancestral, tutelary, totemistic or occupational divinities. Beliefs may be unclear, but non-participation in the relevant occasional and seasonal rites is more or less unthinkable. Cf 1.9.7.

2.1.1 Village religion in Japan

. . . the village shrine and temple serve all the villagers, and the subdivided village shrines and temples serve only the villagers of the subdivision . . .

This concept is seen most clearly in a small island village and isolated community. Hime-shima, for example, is an island in the Inland Sea near Kyushu . . .

The village Shinto shrine is Hachiman-jinja, situated in the middle of the main village, and all the villagers of the island are obliged to serve it . . .

These three eastern hamlets have their particular sub-village shrine, Himekoso-jinja on the seashore in the eastern part of the island, which is attended primarily by the villagers of these three hamlets . . .

On the eastern part of the island in Inazumi hamlet, nine Nakabori families form one family (dōzoku) group which consists of a main family, two sub-main families, and six branch families. The main family has an Izushima-myōjin shrine (enshrining a kami of water or of the sea); one of the sub-main families has an Inari shrine, the other a Kōjin shrine. All members of this family group participate in the annual festivals in the second and eighth months of the lunar calendar and serve these kami. Thus, for example, Matasaku Nakabori, who is a member of the branch family, must join in the festivals of the Kōjin shrine (sub-main family's shrine), and Izushima-myōjin shrine (main family's shrine), the Himekoso-jinja (sub-village shrine), and the Hachiman-jinja (main village shrine). Ichiro Hori. *Folk Religion in Japan, Continuity and Change* (Chicago 1968), 59-61 (edited to avoid too much Japanese terminology)

This account illustrates the principle of simple group religion with regard to detailed kinship groups. It must be admitted however that the *ujigami* system, each *uji* (clan or 'family') having its own *kami* (god), is extremely difficult to document, simply because historically the religious situation has become more complex. The Hachiman cult, for example, spread from place to place, and Hori also mentions a Buddhist (Shingon) temple in Omi hamlet, which has nothing to do with the system.

2.1.2 Deities and caste

Most of the deities honoured at these shrines are also associated with particular castes; a member of the caste serves as priest at the shrine of his castes deity, and the caste group observes a ritual cult of the deity. The shrine to Shitala (smallpox goddess), for instance, is located in the Balai ward by the village pond, a Balai serves as priest and oracle to the goddess, and every year in the month of *Kuar,* the Balai observe a nine day festival in honour of Shitala. The shrine of Ram Deo Ji, a deity of the Bhambi caste, is situated in the Bhambi ward, and a man of the Bhambi caste serves as priest and minstrel at this shrine. The Desha Chamar have the shrine of their caste deity, Bhawani Mata, in a small hut situated in their ward; the deity is served by a Desha Chamar, who observe a seven-day festival of the goddess in the month of *Chait.* K. S. Mathur. 'The Meaning of Hinduism in Rural Malwa' in L. P. Viyarthi (ed). *Aspects of Religion in Indian Society* (Meerut 1961), 116

2.1.3 A Dinka clan divinity

The tree called *rual* is a very great divinity for three descent groups: Parum, Pakwin and Pabuol. Parum is very great throughout Rek country, followed by Pabuol. Pakwin is great in the land of the Malwal Giernyang.

The three descent groups came out from the three children of one wife; Akwin, and Rum, and their sister called Abuol. Parum are the children of Rum, Pakwin are the children of Akwin, and Pabuol are the children of Abuol their sister.

These three descent groups keep cattle dedicated to *Rual* at the central hearth. The rope with which the cow of *Rual* is tethered is decorated with rings, and the milk of this cow is not drunk by any other man, any mere stranger. If it is a man from one of these three descent groups, he will drink. These descent groups do not marry between themselves, for if they do so, they are injured by [the disease brought by] incest. They have other divinities which they respect, but I write only of *Rual.*

A man who is related to *Rual* will not cut down the fruit of the *rual* tree; if he does so, he will become blind. Tiny children are strongly forbidden to play with the fruits of the *rual* tree. The mother of a child of *Rual* also very much respects the *rual* tree because of her child, but not because she is related to *Rual*. G. Lienhardt. *Divinity and Experience, The Religion of the Dinka* (Oxford 1961), 123

The account was actually written by a young Dinka.

2.2 CIVIL RELIGION

Civil religion is the established or official religion of a complex society. The members of such a society may also belong to smaller associations of various kinds, and some may even dissent from the civil religion, possibly reaping not inconsiderable opprobrium thereby. It is difficult to think of any society which is completely devoid of such civil religion, whatever the precise legal position may be with regard to establishment, secularism, religious education, freedom allowed to minor group religions, and so on. Although not otherwise adduced below, Marx-Leninism in the Soviet Union, etc, and Maoism in China should certainly be counted as civil religion. In general, cf also 5.3, 5.6, 5.7, 6.4 and 6.5.

2.2.1 The funeral of Marshal Juin

Alphonse Juin, the three hundred and thirty-ninth Marshal of France, was buried today in the crypt of Saint-Louis des Invalides and a chapter of French history with him.

The gendarme's son from Algeria, who headed his year at St Cyr, served under Lyautey, and fought on the Marne in the action in which Peguy was killed, lived to lead a new-born French Army to the triumph of Garigliano and to earn from Eisenhower the tribute that he was the only French General who had been able to adapt the principles of Napoleon to modern warfare.

The parade which accompanied his coffin to Napoleon's church, where he lies with Leclerc and McMahon and Rouget de Lisle, symbolised his long career. At its head were the white plumes of St Cyr, and the black tricornes of the Polytechnique. The tanks roared behind, and above, in a last salute, flashed Mirages and Fouga Magisters, trailing behind them bands of blue, white, and red smoke.

Over the weekend Marshal Juin had lain in state in the Church of Saint-Louis, where it is estimated that 200,000 people filed past his coffin. Among them was the former General Zeller, recently pardoned by General de Gaulle after his part in the Algerian putsch.

Au revoir

Shortly after 1 am today the coffin was taken to Notre Dame, where relays of officers mounted guard around it through the night. The first and most moving part of the State funeral took place there when, at 10am, Mgr Badre, Chaplain to the Forces, celebrated the requiem mass before an overflowing congregation headed by General and Mme de Gaulle.

At the end of it Cardinal Feltin, former Archbishop of Paris, looking out over the ranks of uniforms, reminded his heroes that the great soldier to whom the Church was rendering these final duties, was also a great Christian. That being so, the Cardinal's last words to his old friend were: 'Monsieur le maréchal, au revoir.'

The temporal pomp began outside the West door of the cathedral, where the crowd lined the square three or four feet deep as they lined the whole of the long reach past the Hôtel de Ville up the Rue de Rivoli, across the Concorde, up the Champs-Elysées, and finally left along Avenue Winston Churchill and over the river.

The Marshal's coffin, covered with a gold-fringed tricolour, was placed on a gun carriage drawn by eight bays. On it were laid the tunic which he had worn during the Italian campaign and his kepi wreathed with gold oak leaves. Four Generals were the pall-bearers. Four officers following carried the blue

Marshal's baton, glittering with stars, and his 39 decorations arrayed on crimson cushions. Pacing slowly to the inexorable beat of the funeral marches, Chopin, Beethoven, Mendelssohn, and the thudding of black-draped drums, the procession took half an hour to pass.

The parade

General de Gaulle did not walk with the cortége, but rejoined it at Les Invalides. Mme Juin, frail and heavily veiled, with her two sons and other members of the family, did.

For the rest, there was virtually France and a host of friendly countries. M. Pompidou led a group of Ministers. The endless uniformed files included Lord Alexander of Tunis, representing the British Government and also the Order of the Bath, of which Marshal Juin was a Knight of the Grand Cross; General Lemnitzer, Commander-in-Chief, Allied Forces, Europe; Rear-Admiral Wainwright, representing British Armed Forces; and General Boehmler, who commanded a German parachute division at Monte Cassino.

The representatives of the Forces were almost equalled in numbers by detachments of ex-servicemen bearing the colours often of regiments now disbanded.

At Les Invalides, M. Messler, Minister of the Armed Forces, pronounced the eulogy. After recapitulating the events of Marshal Juin's career, he added that for history the Marshal was the victor of Garigliano. Nesta Roberts. 'Last salute to a great soldier', *Guardian*, 2 February 1967

2.2.2 Civil religion in Lancaster

Earlier, the new High Sheriff, who recently succeded Colonel H. J. Darlington of Halton, had taken part in the traditional ceremonial before the opening of the Assize.

A service at Lancaster Priory was attended by the Judge, Mr Justice Bridge; the Mayor of Lancaster, Alderman S. J. Smith; Town Clerk, Mr J. D. Waddell; the Lord Lieutenant of Lancashire, Lord Rhodes; Chief Constable of the County, Mr

W. J. H. Palfrey; Police Superintendent B. Spence; Chief Inspector W. Eva; the High Sheriff and Colonel Darlington.

The service was conducted by the Rev Paul Warren, curate at the Priory and Anglican Chaplain at Lancaster University.

Singing was led by the Priory Choir and pupils of Ripley St Thomas C.E. Secondary School were also among the congregation.

The arrival and departure of the Judge's procession was heralded by a fanfare played by members of the Lancashire Constabulary Band.

The Mayor, Town Clerk and Beadle, Mr R. Dennison, led the Judge's procession to the Castle, watched by a small crowd. Before the service the Mayor, the Town Clerk, Mr Palfrey and Superintendent Spence paid a courtesy call on the Judge at the Judge's Lodgings. *The Lancaster Guardian,* Friday 14 May 1971 (Lancaster)

One can only speculate as to why the pupils of St Thomas Church of England Secondary School were present at the Church, but no doubt they were impressed by the ceremonial splendour of the moral authorities. The Castle, at the side of which the Priory Church is to be found, contains courtrooms and prison accommodation, and another of the curates makes regular visits to the prisoners.

2.2.3 Imperial rescript on education

Know ye, our subjects :

Our Imperial Ancestors have founded Our Empire on a basis broad and everlasting, and have deeply and firmly implanted virtue; Our subjects ever united in loyalty and filial piety have from generation to generation illustrated the beauty thereof. This is the glory of the fundamental character of Our Empire, and herein also lies the source of Our Education. Ye, our subjects, be filial to your parents, affectionate to your brothers and sisters; as husbands and wives be harmonious; as

F

friends true; bear yourselves in modesty and moderation; extend your benevolence to all; pursue learning and cultivate arts, and thereby develop intellectual faculties and perfect moral powers; furthermore, advance public good and promote common interests; always respect the Constitution and observe the laws; should emergency arise, offer yourselves courageously to the State; and thus guard and maintain the prosperity of Our Imperial Throne coeval with heaven and earth. So shall ye not only be our good and faithful subjects, but render illustrious the best traditions of your forefathers.

The Way here set forth is indeed the teaching bequeathed by Our Imperial Ancestors, to be observed alike by Their Descendants and subjects, infallible for all ages and true in all places. It is Our wish to lay it to heart in all reverence, in common with you, Our subjects, that we may all attain to the same virtue. R. Tsunoda (ed). *Sources of Japanese Tradition* (New York 1958), 646-7

This rescript was promulgated under the Emperor Meiji in 1890 and was read daily in Japanese schools until 1945.

2.2.4 The pledge of allegiance

I pledge allegiance to the flag of the United States of America and to the Republic for which it stands, one nation, under God, indivisable, with liberty and justice for all. (Quoted from oral tradition)

This pledge is recited daily by American schoolchildren.

2.3 FOLK RELIGION

'Folk religion' is used here to refer to miscellaneous and incidental religious behaviour which does not involve the person concerned in a coherent religious grouping of any kind. (This is not to say that persons individually so involved may not in fact form some other sociologically discernible group; eg those who do not walk under ladders *might* all be the third cousins of house-painters and tilers.) The phrase 'folk religion' is sometimes used more widely to refer to religions which have not achieved fame. However, many little known cults may be in fact the religions of specific groups, thus falling into one of the categories 'simple group religion' or 'minor group religion'. Folk religion, in the precise sense intended here, runs through complex societies in a maze of threads, perhaps derived from and contributing to more organised religions, but in itself available to all the people incidentally and in no sense normative for specific religious groups. One might include here such things as 'nature mysticism', residual belief in God, providence, immortality, etc, on the part of persons who have lost all contact with organised religion, the wearing of crosses by avowedly not particularly Christian 'hippies', belief in miscellaneous spirits and ghosts, and the use of horoscopes and similar services provided impersonally through the mass media. One of the borderlines of folk religion is when ad hoc rites or services are offered by specialists who themselves *are* linked with a coherent religious group, while the beneficiaries or customers are not. Divination and astrology have frequently fallen in this ambiguous area.

2.3.1 Miscellaneous folk religion

'Home to meet a ghost. Rating flown from Malta.' His wife was troubled by a black and white phantom without a head, who punched her three young children . . .

'Workers pray to stop a hoodoo.' Two directors and a foreman had died suddenly at work. The minister is quoted as saying, 'The men in the factory who fear a hoodoo are really tough, hardy types' . . .

'Canon E.B., of Oxford, said that he had a profound belief in angels, and therefore, in devils or evil spirits. He believed that many patients in our hospitals were really possessed by demons rather than suffering from diseases of the mind.' Report of a speech at the Convocation of Canterbury . . .

'We paid gipsy £1,400 to lift spells, say women.' The gipsy claimed to be the seventh child of a seventh child, with second sight. She promised to restore the ladies' fortunes by 'turning the planets' . . .

'Marriage advice "swindle".' A Moscow housewife ran a 'save your marriage' mail order service, promising to restore harmany. According to *Pravda* the cure consisted of taking an ordinary piece of paper, folding it, and putting it near one's bed. An alarm must be set for midnight, and when it rings one tears a strip off the paper. The operation is to be repeated if necessary, and if it still fails one can throw earth out of the window or burn a few of one's hairs. Gustav Jahoda. *The Psychology of Superstition* (1969), 19-20

The cases are quoted and summarised from various newspapers.

2.4 MINOR GROUP RELIGION

A 'minor group religion' is the religion of a coherent group within a more complex society, or perhaps drawn from several such complex societies as in 2.4.4 and 2.4.5. Such religions are extremely varied with regard to their beliefs and practices, and it is unfortunate that attempts to categorise them in greater detail into 'denominations' and 'sects' or 'sects' and 'cults' have been based largely on the doctrines taught while the religions considered have been mainly drawn from the western world. This means that typologies suggested have only been of limited value, as was found, for example, by James Allen Dator in his book *The Soka Gakkai* (Washington 1969), in which he tried to apply them to a Japanese case. A recent general discussion of the problem is available in Roland Robertson's *The Sociological Interpretation of Religion* (Oxford 1970). The development of a generally relevant typology would involve two distinct steps as a start : firstly a categorisation based on variations in the actual form of association among the members, and secondly a more complex comparison correlating types of association with types of conceptual system (cf 5.6). To be complete, the other two main aspects basic to any religious data would then also have to be taken into account, and finally other relevant sociological and psychological factors would have to be adduced. Such a task falls far beyond the scope of the present exercise. The cases adduced below simply have in common the fact that the associated members are drawn together from within the major natural groups to which they otherwise belong. Three of them indicate a conscious appeal to a limited, special clientele and suggest where their support actually comes from.

2.4.1 The community at Qumran

This is the procedure which all members of the community are to follow in dealings with one another, wherever they dwell.

Everyone is to obey his superior in rank in all matters of work or money. But all are to dine together, worship together and take counsel together.

Wherever there be ten men who have been formally enrolled in the community, one who is a priest is not to depart from them. When they sit in his presence, they are to take their places according to their respective ranks; and the same order is to obtain when they meet for common counsel.

When they set the table for a meal or prepare wine to drink, the priest is first to put his hand forth to invoke a blessing on the first portion of the bread or wine.

Similarly, wherever there be ten men who have been formally enrolled in the community, there is not to be absent from them one who can interpret the Law to them at any time of day or night, for the harmonious adjustment of their human relations.

The general members of the community are to keep awake for a third of all the nights of the year reading books, studying the Law and worshipping together. Theodor H. Gaster (trans). *The Dead Sea Scriptures* (New York 1956) 49-50 (*The Manual of Discipline* vi, 1-8)

Cf 5.7.3, 5.7.4 and 5.7.5.

2.4.2   The type of person who became a Christian

Divine folly is wiser than the wisdom of man, and divine weakness stronger than man's strength. My brothers, think what sort of people you are, whom God has called. Few of you are men of wisdom, by any human standard; few are powerful or highly born. Yet, to shame the wise, God has chosen what the world counts folly, and to shame what is strong, God has chosen what the world counts weakness. He has chosen things low and contemptible, mere nothings, to overthrow the existing order. And so there is no place for human pride in the presence of God.
1 Corinthians i, 25-9

Other aspects of the communal life of Christians are evidenced in other parts of this epistle of Paul. In the early period Christians were drawn from various strata of society, but mainly the lower.

2.4.3   The Mantis Health School

This cult's activity is centred in one of the apartments in the resettlement area and is called the Mantis Health School or the Mantis Gymnasium . . .

New members are usually introduced to the cult by other pupils or inquire because of its reputation. The fact that the cult does not actively proselytize is explained by the teacher: 'We do not advertise or propagandise since our forerunners did not.' He emphasised that there is no screening process or admission requirements:

'It's unnecessary because the bad ones would not dare to come. It is hard work and it is very difficult to complete training within a short period of time. Without humility and patience one cannot get anywhere.'

At the time our observers were in the resettlement area there were between twenty and thirty people (both male and female and including several individuals who were from outside the resettlement area) actively involved in learning the traditional arts . . .

When a pupil enters the gymnasium, he pays respect to the

tablets of the Grand Teacher (the founder) and the Earth God. He bows in front of the tablets and places lighted incense sticks on the two shrines . . .

The lessons usually begin by practising the system of movements of the *qi lín* dance. Often the teacher beats the drum himself. At the drummer's left a man strikes a gong; the cymbalist is at his right. During practice exercises, advanced pupils teach the less advanced, the teacher supervises and the dancers change several times in order to allow everyone to participate. Then the pupils perform another set of movements, often the brandishing of a club and sword followed by traditional Chinese boxing. M. I. Berkowitz, F. P. Brandauer and J. H. Reed. 'Folk Religion in an Urban Setting: A Study of Hakka Villagers in Transition', *Ching Feng* XII, 3-4 (Hong Kong 1969), 88-91

The authors use the phrase 'folk religion' to refer to everything other than classical state Confucianism or the 'great tradition' (p 9), ie they use it in a wider sense than is given to it in 2.3 above. *Qi lín,* a fabulous imaginary animal whose appearance is traditionally supposed to precede that of a sage.

2.4.4 Greetings from Auroville

As anticipated in our previous number, on 28 February, amid the enchanted expanse running across Madras-Pondicherry frontiers, on the Bay of Bengal, there bloomed forth a vivacious human flower as thousands of men and women abounded the amphitheatre that girdled a magnificent lotus in mosaic. It was a bright morning. A solemn silence from the assembled multitude greeted, at 10.30 a.m., the words of the Mother carried through a live broadcast, as she spoke from her room in the Sri Aurobindo Ashram, about six miles away. She said:

'Greetings from Auroville to all men of goodwill.

'Are invited to Auroville all those who thirst for progress and aspire to a higher and truer life.'

This message was followed by her reading the Charter of Auroville, and as the reading of the charter went on by others in several languages, young men and women representing all the countries of the world moved in a slow and serene procession pouring into the lotus the symbolic earth of all the lands of the world. Thus was marked the birth of the City of Dawn—Auroville...

The inspiration behind Auroville can best be appreciated in the light of Sri Aurobindo's vision of the future of man. His and the Mother's is the profoundest optimism. They envision man as an evolving being for whom there awaits a glorious future when this 'earth shall be the Spirit's manifest home'. The realisation of an enlightened life includes both the outward exploration of Nature and the inner exploration of consciousness. Auroville will be the place for an experiment in this direction. Then, supremely significant are these words from the charter :

'Auroville belongs to nobody in particular. Auroville belongs to humanity as a whole. But to live in Auroville one must be the willing servitor of the Divine's consciousness.' 'Auroville' (editorial), *World Union* VIII, no 2 (Pondicherry April 1968)

Cf 2.4.5.

2.4.5   The membership of World Union

For carrying on its work, for the realisation of its aims, World Union invites the cooperation of all individuals and organisations that seek to serve the cause of human unity. It welcomes all sources of inspiration for the common cause. It has members, officers, and council members who are seekers and workers of many different affiliations...

We are not interested in nominal memberships. But we are interested in all who are working or who feel an inner urge to work for world unity, either in their small personal circle, in a local or regional World Union centre, or in a wider field of influence... *World Union* (pamphlet, Pondicherry 1968), 11th unnumbered page.

Cf 2.4.4.

2.5 SPECIALISTS IN RELIGION

The various specialists in religion: hermits and holy men, founders and reformers, shamans, shamanesses and prophets, patriarchs, spiritual directors, and so on, may be related to any of the social shapes into which religion may otherwise be seen to fall. A shaman, for example, may be the leading figure in a simply organised society, at other times shamans may operate in the context of minor group religions, or again shamanism may survive in a purely ad hoc manner which would fall under our category of folk religion. Everybody involved in a religion may be said to be a specialist in the sense of having a defined role and not some other. However, the observance of distinctive specialisms raises the question of individual initiative and power in influencing religious activity. To what extent is this 'charisma' to be understood in terms of the prescribed office and to what extent is it dependent on certain individuals themselves?

2.5.1 The specialists and the motley crowd

It may help us in this rather long prayer to picture a vast procession passing before the Throne of God in answer to our petition. Let us watch them:

We see a countless host approaching, and can gradually single them out.

First, a Royal Calvacade, and among them Our own Sovereign, and with him, 'all in authority' under him—The Cabinet, Judges, Generals, Admirals, Air Marshals, M.P.s, Magistrates.

There follows the Church procession—Archbishops, Bishops, Priests—from the highest patriarch to the humblest curate.

Then comes a motley crowd of civilians, amongst whom you can discern 'this congregation here present'—including yourself . . . T. Dilworth-Harrison (Archdeacon and Vicar of Chesterfield). *Every Boy's Confirmation Book* (1950), 50-1

This is part of the commentary on the prayer for 'the whole state of Christ's Church militant here in earth' in the Holy Communion service of the Church of England.

2.5.2   Stations of life and specialists in India

Four are the stations of life, household life, studentship, life of the silent sage, and life in the forest. He who renounces life should go about without any sacrificial rite in fire, without a house, without any enjoyment, without seeking anybody's shelter, opening his mouth only for recital of sacred texts and mantras like OM, taking from the village only so much as will hold his body and soul together, and bereft of any act of this-worldly or other-worldly prospect . . .

The teacher is called *āchārya* because the student gathers from him the dharmas. Never should [a student] think ill of him [the teacher], for the teacher gives him a [new] birth in knowledge, [and] that is the highest birth. Mother and father produce one's body only. Morgan. *The Religion of the Hindus* 325 and 324 (quoting *Āpastamba Dharma Sūtra* VIII, 2 and I, 1. 14-18)

Āchārya is a technical term for the spiritual teacher, and *dharmas* refers not so much to teachings as to the proper path which the student, or disciple, should follow to make spiritual progress.

2.5.3   Teacher of the Mantis Health School

The teacher of the Mantis Health School explained that the practices of the cult originated in a Buddhist monastery, the Temple of Bamboo Wood, in Kiangsi Province. The cult's system has been passed from teacher to pupil for several generations . . . He said that after studying gymnastics for more than ten years, he had studied traditional Chinese medicine. Asked if he thought any of the craft might be lost, since it was passed from generation to generation without the aid of a textbook, he replied : 'When a teacher gets old, he passes on all his craft to his pupils without reservation. Whether or not they learn depends on their individual efforts and intelligence.' It is commonly understood within the community that nobody is qualified to teach until his own teacher authorises him. Berkowitz, Brandauer and Reed. 'Folk Religion in an Urban Setting, A Study of Hakka Villagers in Transition', 88-9

Cf 2.4.3.

2.5.4 A spiritual director

It is a matter of great importance to a soul seeking perfection that it should be directed in its way by a wise priest learned in the spiritual life, but unfortunately such a priest is not very easy to find; we have indeed, many confessors, but few directors . . .

Once the director has visualised the state of the soul and decided upon its way, it is not generally necessary to do more than deal with questions and difficulties as they arise, except at long intervals or when a change occurs in the spiritual state of the soul . . .

The relationship between confessor and penitent or director and directed is so intimate, being concerned with the deepest things of the spirit, that it creates a real bond between them, and when that bond is truly spiritual and in God, it is right and good; the difficulty is that it is apt to become, on the penitent's side, at least, something merely emotional. This can be counteracted by real detachment on the part of the priest, who should also train his child in this fundamental austerity. Harton. *The Elements of the Spiritual Life : A Study in Ascetical Theology*, 335-7

2.5.5 Pimiko the shamaness

. . . the country of Wa [Japan] was in a state of great confusion, war and conflict raging on all sides. For a number of years there was no ruler. Then a woman named Pimiko appeared. Remaining unmarried, she occupied herself with magic and sorcery, and bewitched the populace. Thereupon they placed her on the throne. She kept one thousand female attendants, but few people saw her. There was only one man who was in charge of her

wardrobe and meals and acted as the medium of communication. She resided in a palace surrounded by towers and stockade,
with the protection of armed guards. The laws and customs
were strict and stern. Tsunoda. *Sources of Japanese Tradition,*
9. This passage adapted from Tsunoda and Goodrich, *Japan in
the Chinese Dynastic Histories* (South Pasadena 1951), 1-3

2.5.6   Elijah, Elisha and the sons of the prophets

Then Eli'jah said to him, 'Tarry here, I pray you; for the Lord
has sent me to the Jordan.' But he said, 'As the Lord lives, and
as you yourself live, I will not leave you.' So the two of them
went on. Fifty men of the sons of the prophets also went, and
stood at some distance from them, as they both were standing
by the Jordan. Then Eli'jah took his mantle, and rolled it up,
and struck the water, and the water was parted to the one side
and to the other, till the two of them could go over on dry
ground.

When they had crossed, Eli'jah said to Eli'sha, 'Ask what I
shall do for you, before I am taken from you.' And Eli'sha said,
'I pray you, let me inherit a double share of your spirit.' And
he said, 'You have asked a hard thing; yet, if you see me as I
am being taken from you, it shall be so for you; but if you do
not see me, it shall not be so.' And as they still went on and
talked, behold, a chariot of fire and horses of fire separated the
two of them. And Eli'jah went up by a whirlwind into heaven.
And Eli'sha saw it and he cried, 'My father, my father! the
chariots of Israel and its horsemen!' And he saw him no more.

Then he took hold of his own clothes and rent them in two
pieces. And he took up the mantle of Eli'jah that had fallen from
him, and went back and stood on the bank of the Jordan. Then
he took the mantle of Eli'jah that had fallen from him, and
struck the water, saying, 'Where is the Lord, the God of Eli'jah?'
And when he had struck the water, the water was parted to the
one side and to the other; and Eli'sha went over . . .

He went up from there to Bethel; and while he was going up
on the way, some small boys came out of the city and jeered at

him, saying, 'Go up, you baldhead! Go up, you baldhead!' And he turned around, and when he saw them, he cursed them in the name of the Lord. And two she-bears came out of the woods and tore forty-two of the boys. 2 Kings ii, 6-24

Although details of the social organisation of prophecy in ancient Israel remain obscure, this extract illustrates that there were both recognisable groups of prophets and more or less isolated, revered, and despised individuals.

PART THREE

Religious States of Mind

I f religion has a varied social shape, the states of mind experienced by individuals are no less diverse. Moreover it is extremely difficult to study such states of mind systematically and comparatively without immediately raising behavioural, sociological and doctrinal questions. Although the subject has fascinated various writers in the past, there is no satisfactory account of it, and the following pages by no means claim to offer one. The classic work remains William James' *The Varieties of Religious Experience,* written as long ago as 1901-2. Read today, it suffers through being mainly western-orientated, perhaps also through over-reliance on special, even abnormal, cases and through entanglement in associated but not immediately relevant problems. Another epoch-making work in this area was Rudolf Otto's *The Idea of the Holy* (1923 originally *Das Heilige* 1917), which demonstrated the importance of the sense of 'the numinous' as a fundamental type of religious experience. It may be noted that Otto was more concerned with discussing the place of the irrational element in religious experience within a satisfactory (Christian) philosophy of religion than with attempting a systematic phenomenological study of religious feeling.

The special subject of 'mysticism' has attracted a good deal of attention, about which a little more will be said later. At first sight it may seem appropriate to draw a major distinction between such energetic persons as Amos, Nichiren, and other charismatic religious leaders, and quiet contemplatives such as

Eckhart, al-Hallāj, Mahāvīra and the Buddha, thus giving a neat typology of 'prophetic' and 'mystical' religious experience. This would however be much too simple. For one thing, neither prophetism nor mysticism can be regarded only as religious states, but have to be seen also in terms of their place within given religious traditions, etc. Secondly, the greater the number of individual cases adduced the less satisfactory the polarised distinction seems to be: What about Hosea, for example, or what about Hōnen? What about Thomas à Kempis, Bunyan or Kierkegaard? Thirdly, Otto's account of the experience of 'the numinous' straddles any too simple typology, and its relationship to the experience of the prophet and of the mystic respectively is not easy to clarify. Fourthly, there is a greater variety of religious states of mind than can possibly be subsumed under these two heads. Consider for example the experience of alienation and restoration, possession and automatism, disciplined self-giving in moral, charitable or political works, states of devotional or sacramental elation, and persistent self-mortification in the desert, in the forest or in the kitchen. The mere listing of these shows that some differentiation between types of religious states is both possible and desirable; however, this has not yet been achieved in a manner which is both tidy and satisfactory. Moreover the frequent interplay between different types seems to demand a much more complex grid than has hitherto been offered. For these reasons the sub-categorisation which follows here is very loosely designed.

Mention should be made of a rather different way in which religious states could be schematised, namely, in terms of 'the moral element', 'the rational element', 'the affective element', etc, as delineated in R. H. Thouless' *An Introduction to the Psychology of Religion* (Cambridge 1923). Such a principle might at first sight be thought to be more happily complementary to the way in which religious groups were categorised above. However since Thouless was on the whole more concerned with the relationship between religious and non-religious factors, it seemed more appropriate at this point to follow a path more in line with the phenomenology of religion as generally understood, and to make use of categories which fit more closely with the self-understanding of religious persons themselves.

3.1 ALIENATION AND CONVERSION

While there are those fortunate enough to enjoy 'the religion of healthy-mindedness', to use the famous expression of William James, there are also those whose experience is that of 'the sick soul' or of 'the divided self'. Here belong the feeling of ideological homelessness or the sense that things are utterly meaningless, even malignantly so, and also moral maladjustment and the 'conviction' of one's depravity or sinfulness, or again, in eastern terms, the realisation of one's slavery to the passions and the never-ending round of birth and death. The counterpoint to such states of mind frequently lies already within them and finds expression in an appropriate form of 'conversion'. Such states are also routinised in ritual confession and renewal, etc. A full treatment should consider also the phenomenon of loss of belief. Wider sociological aspects of 'alienation' and 'conversion' are of course not considered here; nor indeed is the problem of conversion from one religion to another, which is a much wider subject.

3.1.1 Decision and forgiveness

Knowledge of sin had ripened into the sense of sin; at church one sentence in the sermon had caught my attention, though I was usually inattentive. The impression faded away immediately. Two days later, while in business, there was a sudden arrest of my thought without a consciously associated natural cause. My whole inner nature seemed summoned to a decision for or against God; and in five minutes I had a distinctly formed

G

purpose to seek Him. It was followed immediately by a change, the principal manifestation of which was a willingness to make known my decision and hope of divine forgiveness . . .

On the impulse of the moment I went to the altar. After an hour of pleading and prayer, I felt something go from me, which seemed like a burden lifted, and something seemed floating nearer and nearer just above me. Suddenly I felt a touch as of the Divine One, and a voice said, 'Thy sins are forgiven thee; arise, go in peace.' . . .

I felt self-condemnation at having done wrong. At the end of ten days I went into my bedroom and prayed. 'Jesus, take me,' is all I said. As I rose and walked across the room it came to me that I was sincere and my prayer was real, and I believed my acceptance with God. Edwin Diller Starbuck. *The Psychology of Religion, An Empirical Study of the Growth of Religious Consciousness* 1901), 107, 79 and 106

These are but three of many cases studied by Starbuck.

3.1.2 The Buddha's disgust and resolution

Thus the Bodhisattva, leaving behind him his great army of elephants, cavalry and footsoldiers, his great stores of wealth, his great sovereignty and his great family, went forth from home into the homeless state. The Bodhisattva, oppressed by birth, went forth from home into the homeless state in order to attain the way that leads beyond birth. Oppressed by death, he went forth from home into the homeless state in order to attain the way that leads beyond death. Oppressed by sorrows and tribulations, he went forth from home into the homeless state in order to attain the way that leads beyond tribulations.

And, monks, it was not when he was worn out with decay that the Bodhisattva went forth from home into the homeless state, but it was when he was in the prime and perfection of his youth. Again, monks, it was not when he was worn out by disease and decay that the Bodhisattva went forth from home into the homeless state, but it was when he was in the prime and perfection of his health. Again, monks, it was not when he was worn out by the loss of wealth that the Bodhisattva went forth from home into the homeless state, but he left behind him a great store of riches. Again, monks, it was not when he was worn out by the loss of his kinsmen that the Bodhisattva went forth from home into the homeless state, but he left behind him a large family of relations. J. J. Jones (trans). *The Mahāvastu* Vol 2 (1952), 157

This account is of course completely stylised but it represents both a summary of and a prescription for religious states of mind both in Indian religions generally and in Buddhism beyond India.

3.1.3 Karma and enlightenment

To lose one's father in those days was perhaps an even greater loss than it is now, for so much depended on him as head of the family—all the important steps in life such as education and finding a position in life afterwards. All this I lost, and by the time I was about seventeen or eighteen these misfortunes made me start thinking about my karma. Why should I have these disadvantages at the very start of life?

My thoughts then started to turn to philosophy and religion, and as my father belonged to the Rinzai sect of Zen it was natural that I should look to Zen for some of the answers to my problems . . .

There followed for me four years of struggle, a struggle mental, physical, moral and intellectual. I felt it must be ultimately quite simple to understand *Mu*, but how was I to take hold of this simple thing? It might be in a book . . .

One of the examples I found in this book I thought I must try to follow. It said, 'When you have enough faith, then you have enough doubt. And when you have enough doubt, then you have enough satori. All the knowledge and experience and wonderful phrases and feelings of pride which you accumulated before your study of Zen—all these things you must throw out. Pour all your mental force onto solving the kōan. Sit up straight regardless of day and night, concentrating your mind on the kōan. When you have been doing this for some time you will find yourself in timelessness and spacelessness like a dead man. When you reach that state something starts up within yourself and suddenly it is as though your skull were broken in pieces. The experience that you gain then has not come from outside, but from within yourself.' . . .

Up till then I had always been conscious that *Mu* was in my mind. But so long as I was conscious of *Mu* it meant that I was somehow separate from *Mu,* and that is not a true *samādhi.* But towards the end of that *sesshin* about the fifth day, I ceased to be conscious of *Mu.* I was one with *Mu,* identified with *Mu,* so that there was no longer the separateness implied by being conscious of *Mu.* This is the real state of *samādhi.* . . . When I came out of that state of *samādhi* during that *sesshin* I said, 'I see. This is it.' Daisetz Teitaro Suzuki. *The Training of the Zen Buddhist Monk* (New York, 1965), xi, xii, xviii, xix, xxi, xxii

Suzuki's personal development described here extended over more than the four years mentioned in the contracted text above. '*Mu*', literally meaning 'nothing' or 'not', is one of the *kōan* (intellectual – spiritual problems) which Suzuki was set by his masters. The book mentioned is a Chinese collection entitled (in Japanese) *Zenkan Sakushin,* and the quotation provides, for our purposes, an example within an example. This whole account of Suzuki's experience was prepared by Miss Mihoko Oka-mura and Dr Carmen Blacker on the basis of interviews, and first published in *The Middle Way* (November 1964). (Hence it does not appear in earlier editions of Suzuki's book.)

───────

3.2 SELF-GIVING

Under this heading are given cases of devotional or 'affective' self-giving and of ascetic self-giving. James has attempted a more detailed categorisation of the latter (*The Varieties of Religious Experience* 291-2). One could speak also of 'rational' self-giving, the sacrifice and/or dedication of the intellect; of the closely connected submission of the will in obedience (cf James, 305); of 'moral' self-giving, which is common to almost all religion, and which has various charitable and political outworkings (cf 1.9); and of willing suffering and martydrom (cf 5.8). All of these have in common that the self is given over to the higher end or sense of the religion in question, whether briefly and passionately or steadily in the long term. The strength of this drive, which often may seem to run quite counter to ordinarily expected individual self-interest, should never be underestimated.

3.2.1 Hindu bhakti

> I ask not kin, nor name, nor place,
>> Nor learned men's society.
> Men's lore for me no value has;
>> Kuttālam's lord, I come to thee.
> Wilt thou one boon on me bestow,
>> A heart to melt in longing sweet,
> As yearns o'er new-born calf the cow,
>> In yearning for thy sacred feet?

I had no virtue, penance, knowledge, self-control. A doll to turn

At another's will I danced, whirled, fell. But me he filled in every limb

With love's mad longing, and that I might climb there whence is no return,

He showed his beauty, made me his. Ah me, when shall I go to him?

Fool's friend was I, none such may know
　　The way of freedom; yet to me
He shew'd the path of love, that so
　　Fruit of past deeds might ended be.
Cleansing my mind so foul, he made me like a god.
Ah who could win that which the Father hath bestowed? . . .
R. C. Zaehner. *Hinduism* (Oxford 1962), 133-4

A hymn of Mānikka Vāśagar, a Tamil Śaivite saint of the ninth century. *Bhakti* means self-surrendering, devotional reliance on the divine.

3.2.2　Christian bhakti

Jesu, Lover of my soul,
　　Let me to thy bosom fly,
While the nearer waters roll,
　　While the tempest still is high :
Hide me, O my Saviour, hide,
　　Till the storm of life be past !
Safe into the haven guide,
　　O receive my soul at last !

Other refuge have I none,
　　Hangs my helpless soul on Thee;
Leave, ah ! leave me not alone,
　　Still support and comfort me :
All my trust on Thee is stayed,
　　All my help from Thee I bring;
Cover my defenceless head
　　With the shadow of Thy wing.

Plenteous grace with Thee is found,
　　Grace to cover all my sin;
Let the healing streams abound,
　　Make and keep me pure within :

Thou of life the Fountain art,
Freely let me take of Thee,
Spring Thou up within my heart,
Rise to all eternity.
The Methodist Hymn-book (1904), Hymn 106

Hymn by Charles Wesley.

3.2.3 Giving away the self

Amida's revelation is not to be sought after by our own efforts; it comes upon us by itself, of its own accord. Amida is always in us and with us, but by means of our human understanding we posit him outside us, against us, as opposing us, and exercise our intellectual power to the utmost to take hold of him. The revelation, however, would only take place when this human power has been really exhausted, has given up all its selfishness, when we have come back to our *simplicity*. We can only *feel* him as Heart of our heart and Spirit of our spirit; we can only *feel* him in the love and joy we feel when we give up ourself and stand before him face to face.

The spirit of renunciation is the deepest reality of the human heart. Our self can realise itself truly only by giving itself away. In *giving (dana)* is our truest joy and liberation, for it is uniting ourselves to that extent with the Infinite. We grow by losing ourselves, by uniting. Gaining a thing is by its nature partial, it is limited only to a particular want, but giving is complete, it belongs to our wholeness, it springs not from any necessity but from our affinity with the Infinite, which is the principle of unity and perfection that we have in our inmost heart. Our abiding happiness is not in getting anything, but in giving ourselves up to what is greater than ourselves, to the infinite ideal of perfection. Kenryo Kanamatsu. *Naturalness* (California 1956), 4-5

Amida is the Japanese form of the name Amitābha (Buddha) (cf 3.3.6). *Dana* is the first of the ten perfections.

3.2.4 Self-dedication in the desert

O wasteland bright with the spring flowers of Christ! O solitude out of which come those stones that build the city of the great King in the Apocalypse! O desolate desert rejoicing in God's familiar presence! What keeps you in the world, O brother? You are above and beyond the world. How long is the shade of a house going to conceal you? How long shall the grimy prisons of those cities intern you? Believe me, out here I see more light than you; and how wonderful it is, flinging aside the weight of the body to fly into the pure radiant sky! Are you afraid of proverty? Christ calls the poor blessed. Or does strenuous work frighten you? Without sweat no athlete wins trophies. Worried about lack of food? Faith never feels the pangs of hunger. Do you fear that the bare ground will bruise a body emaciated by fasting? The Lord lies there on the ground beside you. Filthy, long hair horrifies you? Your head is Christ. The desert's infinite vastness terrifies you? In the spirit you may stroll in Paradise : as often as you ascend there in contemplation, so often shall you leave the desert. But your skin attracts mange because one never bathes out here? Once you have been washed in Christ you need no other bath.

To all these complaints the Apostle gives one brief reply, 'The sufferings of this present time are not worthy to be comppared with the glory which shall come, and which shall be revealed in us.' You are a spoiled, pampered man indeed, my dearest Heliodorus, if you desire both to rejoice here in this world and then to reign afterwards with Christ. Paul Carroll. *The Satirical Letters of St Jerome* (Chicago 1956), 13-14 (Letter from The Desert of Chalcis, AD 374)

3.2.5 Ascetic renunciation in Jainism

By renouncing pleasures he [the soul] obtains freedom from false longing, whereby he becomes compassionate, humble, free from sorrow, and destroys the Karman produced by delusion regarding conduct . . .

By renouncing activity he obtains inactivity, by ceasing to act

he acquires no new Karman, and destroys the Karman he had
acquired before . . .

By renouncing company he obtains singleness; being single
and concentrating his mind, he avoids disputes, quarrels,
passions, and censoriousness, and he acquires a high degree of
control . . .

By renouncing all food he prevents his being born again many
hundreds of times.

By perfect renunciation he enters the final [fourth stage of
pure meditation], whence there is no return . . . Hermann
Jacobi. *Jaina Sûtras* Part II. Müller (ed). Sacred Books of the
East XLV (Oxford 1895), 166-8

3.3 EXPERIENCE OF POWER AND PRESENCE

Rudolf Otto used the word 'numinous' to refer to a state of
mind which is *sui generis* and not definable in non-religious
terms (*The Idea of the Holy*, 21). This mental state typically
involves the sense of a mysterious, overwhelming, wholly other
power, which it at one and the same time both terrifying and
fascinating. Otto covered an extremely wide spectrum of cases
with this concept, and though he emphasised the element of
'awefulness' and 'horror' as of ghosts or demons, he also
wrote, 'The feeling of it may at times come sweeping like a
gentle tide, pervading the mind with a tranquil mood of
deepest worship.' (*The Idea of the Holy*, 26). The first three
cases below are adduced by Otto himself.

3.3.1 Luther on the majesty of God

Yea, He is more terrible and frightful than the Devil. For He
dealeth with us and bringeth us to ruin with power, smiteth
and hammereth us and payeth no heed to us . . . In his majesty
He is a consuming fire . . . For therefrom can no man refrain:
if he thinketh on God aright, his heart in his body is struck with
terror . . . Yea, as soon as he heareth God named, he is filled

with trepidation and fear. Rudolf Otto. *The Idea of the Holy* (1959), 115 (quoting Luther's sermon on Exodus xx)

Otto notes in this context that he drew upon his knowledge of Luther's terminology when singling out 'majesty' and 'fear' as notes within the 'numinous' experience.

3.3.2 The burden of St John of the Cross

As this clear sight of the divine comes like a violent assault upon the soul to subdue it, the soul feels such anguish in its weakness that all power and breath leave it together, while sense and spirit as though they stood burdened beneath a dark unmeasured load suffer such agony and are oppressed by such deadly fear that the soul would choose death as a mitigation and refreshment . . .

Therefore he destroys, crushes and overwhelms (the soul) in such a deep darkness, that it feels as though melted and in its misery destroyed by a cruel death of the spirit. Even as though it were to feel it had been swallowed by some savage beast and buried in the darkness of his belly. Otto. *The Idea of the Holy,* 122 (quoting St John of the Cross, *The Ascent of Mount Carmel*)

3.3.3 Arjuna sees God

Arjuna said :

O God, the gods in your body I behold and all the hosts of every kind of being; Brahmā, the lord, [I see] throned on the lotus-seat, celestial serpents and all the [ancient] seers. Arms, bellies, mouths and eyes all manifold—so do I see You wherever I may look—infinite your form! End, middle, or again beginning I cannot see in You, O Monarch Universal, [manifest] in every form! Yours the crown, the mace, the discus—a mass of glory shining on all sides—so do I see You—yet how hard are You to see,—for on every side there is brilliant light of fire and sun. Oh, who should comprehend it? You are the Imperishable, [You] wisdom's highest goal; You, of this universe the last prop-and-resting-place, You the changeless, [You] the guardian of eternal law, You the primeval Person; [at last] I understand. Beginning, middle, or end You do not know,—how infinite your strength! How numberless your arms,—your eyes the sun and moon! So do I see You,—your mouth a flaming fire, burning up this whole universe with your blazing glory. By You alone is this space between heaven and earth pervaded,—all points of the compass too; gazing on this, your marvellous, frightening form, the three worlds shudder, [All-] Highest Self!

Lo! these hosts of gods are entering into You; some, terror-struck, extol You, hands together pressed; great seers and men perfected in serried ranks cry out, 'All hail,' and praise You with copious hymns of praise. Rudras, Ādityas, Vasus, Sādhyas, All-gods, Aśvins, Maruts, and [the ancestors] who quaff the steam, minstrels divine, sprites, demons, and the hosts of perfected saints gaze upon You, all utterly amazed.

Gazing upon your mighty form with its myriad mouths, eyes, arms, thighs, feet, bellies, and sharp, gruesome tusks, the worlds [all] shudder [in affright],—how much more I! Ablaze with many-coloured [flames] You touch the sky, your mouths wide open, [gaping,] your eyes distended, blazing; so do I see You and my inmost self is shaken : I cannot bear it, I find no peace, O Vishnu!

I see your mouths with jagged, ghastly tusks reminding [me] of Time's [devouring] fire : I cannot find my bearings, I cannot find a refuge; have mercy, God of gods, home of the universe!

R. C. Zaehner (trans). *The Bhagavad-Gītā* (Oxford 1969), 83-4

Otto claimed this as a 'classical' passage for his theory of religion.

3.3.4 Sri Ramakrishna's vision of Kāli

And, indeed, he soon discovered what a strange Goddess he had chosen to serve. He became gradually enmeshed in the web of Her all-pervading presence. To the ignorant She is, to be sure, the image of destruction; but he found in Her the benign, all-loving Mother. Her neck is encircled with a garland of heads,

and Her waist with a girdle of human arms, and two of Her
hands hold weapons of death, and Her eyes dart a glance of fire;
but, strangely enough, Ramakrishna felt in Her breath the
soothing touch of tender love and saw in Her the Seed of Immortality. She stands on the bosom of Her Consort, Śiva; it is
because she is the Śakti, the Power, inseparable from the Absolute. She is surrounded by jackals and other unholy creatures,
the denizens of the cremation ground. But is not the Ultimate
Reality above holiness and unholiness? She appears to be reel-
ing under the spell of wine. But who would create this mad
world unless under the influence of a divine drunkenness? She is
the highest symbol of all the forces of nature, the synthesis of
their antinomies, the Ultimate Divine in the form of woman.
She now became to Sri Ramakrishna the only Reality, and the
world became an insubstantial shadow. Into Her worship he
poured his soul. Before him She stood as the transparent portal
to the shrine of Ineffable Reality. Mahendranath Gupta. *The
Gospel of Sri Ramakrishna* (New York 1969, translated from the
Bengali and published by the Ramakrishna-Vivekananda
Center), 12-13 (from the Introduction by Swami Nikhilananda)

3.3.5   Saint Teresa on intellectual vision

When one is not thinking at all of any such favour and has not
even had the idea of meriting it, suddenly one feels at one's side
Our Lord Jesus Christ, *without seeing Him* either with the eyes
of the body or those of the soul. This sort of vision is called intellectual. I do not know why . . . Intellectual visions do not go
quickly, like imaginary ones, but last several days, sometimes
more than a year . . . We know that God is present in all our
actions: but such is the infirmity of our nature, that we often
lose sight of this truth. Here this forgetfulness is impossible, because Our Lord, Who is close to the soul, keeps her constantly
awake: and as she has an almost continual love for That which
she sees, *or rather feels* close to her, she receives the more frequently the favours of which we have spoken. Evelyn Underhill.
Mysticism, A Study in the Nature and Development of Man's

Spiritual Consciousness (1911), 340 (quoting St Teresa, *El Castillo Interior*, Moradas Sextas viii)

3.36 Vision of the Buddha Amitāyus

'Listen carefully! Listen carefully! Think over what you have heard! I, Buddha, am about to explain in detail the law of delivering one's self from trouble and torment. Commit this to your memory in order to explain it in detail before a great assembly.' While Buddha was uttering these words, Buddha Amitāyus stood in the midst of the sky with Bodhisattvas Mahāsthāma and Avalokiteśvara, attending on his right and left respectively. There was such a bright and dazzling radiance that no one could see clearly; the brilliance was a hundred thousand times greater than that of gold . . . Thereupon Vaidehi saw Buddha Amitāyus and approached the World-Honoured One, and worshipped him, touching his feet; and spoke to him as follows: 'O Exalted One! I am now able, by the power of the Budhha, to see Buddha Amitāyus together with the two Bodhisattvas . . .' E. B. Cowell, Max Müller and J. Takakusu. *Buddhist Mahâyâna Sûtras* (Müller (ed). Sacred Books of the East XLIX) (Oxford 1894), Part 2, 175-6 (from Takakusu's translation of the *Amitâyur-Dhyâna-Sûtra*)

Buddha Amitāyus is to be identified with the Buddha Amitābha, whose Buddha-field in the distant west is the focus of devotion in Pure Land Buddhism.

3.4 MYSTICAL STATES AND SIMILAR

'Mysticism' is a field of study in itself (perhaps unfortunately), and one in which there is little agreement about definitions and interpretations. Even in recent years the analysis of mysticism has sometimes been controlled by theological criteria of doubtful relevance, eg in R. C. Zaehner's *Mysticism Sacred and Profane* (Oxford 1961) (cf Ninian Smart's criticisms in 'Interpretation and Mystical Experience' *Religious*

*Studie*s I (1965), 75-87), and also in H. Dumoulin's *The History of Zen Buddhism* (1963). These writers attempt to distinguish 'theistic' or 'supernatural' mysticism from other types. D. T. Suzuki in his *Mysticism Christian and Buddhist* (1957) suggested an essential similarity of experience as between selected Christian mystics, the Zen experience of *satori* ('enlightenment') and life lived in terms of the Pure Land Buddhist invocation of Amitābha Buddha. Indian writers, notably S. Radhakrishnan in various works, and some Islamic writers (cf 4.10.4) also emphasise the fundamental unity of religious states of mind. Such writers should not be naively misunderstood however. Suzuki's approach is not quite unambiguous, and other Buddhists are often concerned to emphasise the special, almost 'final' character of Buddhist experience as compared with various states which religious men might otherwise achieve. Moreover just as a Buddhist might reject Dumoulin's distinction between natural and supernatural mysticism, so Christian theologians discern a dogmatic *parti pris* in the interpretations of Radhakrishnan. In short, this is an excellent example of a field where systematic phenomenological study must achieve freedom from normative presumptions about the nature of religion.

3.4.1 This Self is Brahman

For all this [world] is Brahman. This Self is Brahman. This Self has four quarters.

The waking state, conscious (*prājña*) of what is without, seven-limbed, with nineteen mouths, experiencing what is gross, common to all men (*vaiśvānara*), is the first quarter.

The state of dream, conscious of what is within, seven-limbed, with nineteen mouths, experiencing what is subtle, composed of light (*taijasa*), is the second quarter . . .

The state of deep sleep, unified, a very mass of wisdom (*prajñāna*), composed of bliss, experiencing bliss, with thought as its mouth, wise (*prājña*), is the third quarter.

This is the Lord of all, This the omniscient. This is the Inner Controller : This is the source of all, for it is both the origin and the end of contingent beings.

Conscious (*prājñā*) of neither within nor without, nor of both together, not a mass of wisdom (*prajñāna*), neither wise nor unwise, unseen, one with whom there is no commerce, impalpable, devoid of distinguishing mark, unthinkable, indescribable, its essence the firm conviction of the oneness of itself, bringing all development (*prapañca*) to an end, tranquil and mild, devoid of duality, such do they deem this fourth to be. That is the Self : that is what should be known. R. C. Zaehner (trans). *Hindu Scriptures* (1966), 201 (*Māndūkya Upanishad*, 2-7)

3.4.2 Complete self-realisation in yoga

This [mind-stuff], although diversified by countless subconscious impressions, exists for the sake of another, because its nature is to produce [things as] combinations. For him who sees the distinction, pondering upon his own states-of-being ceases. Then the mind-stuff is borne down to discrimination, onward towards Isolation. In the intervals of this [mind-stuff] there are other presented-ideas [coming] from subliminal-impressions. The escape from these [subliminal-impressions] is described as being like [the escape from] the hindrances. For one who is not usurious even in respect of Elevation, there follows in every case as a result of discriminative discernment the concentration [called] Rain-cloud of [knowable] things. Then follows the cessation of the hindrances and of karma. Then, because of the endlessness of knowledge from which all obscuring defilements have passed away, what is yet to be known amounts to little. When as a result of this the aspects (*guṇa*) have fulfilled their purpose, they attain to the limit of the sequence of mutations. The positive correlate to the moment, recognised as such at the final limit of the mutation, is a sequence. Isolation is the inverse generation of the aspects, no longer provided with a purpose by the Self, or it is the Energy of Intellect grounded in itself. Woods. *The Yoga-system of Patañjali*, xli

This difficult passage is the text only of Patañjali, without any commentary, and is taken from the last part of his work (*Kāivalyapāda*). Cf 1.2.1.

3.4.3 The eight stages of deliverance

'Now these, Ānanda, are the eight stages of Deliverance. Which are they?

'Having one's self external form, one sees [these] forms. This is the first stage.

'Unaware of one's own external form, one sees forms external to one's self. This is the second stage.

' "Lovely!"—with this thought one becomes intent. This is the third stage.

'Passing wholly beyond perceptions of form, all perceptions of sense-reaction dying away, heedless of all perceptions of the manifold, conscious of space as infinite, one enters into and abides in the sphere of space regarded as infinite. This is the fourth stage.

'Passing wholly beyond the sphere of space regarded as infinite, conscious of reason as infinite, one enters into and abides in the sphere of cognition, regarded as infinite. This is the fifth stage.

'Passing wholly beyond the sphere of reason regarded as infinite, conscious of there being nothing whatever, one enters into and abides in the sphere of nothingness. This is the sixth stage.

'Passing wholly beyond the sphere of nothingness, one enters into and abides in the sphere of "neither-consciousness-nor-unconsciousness." This is the seventh stage.

'Passing wholly beyond the sphere of "neither-ideation-nor-non-ideation," one enters into and abides in a state of suspended perception and feeling. This is the eighth stage.

'These, Ānanda, are the eight stages of Deliverance.

'Now when once a brother, Ānanda, has mastered these eight stages of Deliverance in order, and has also mastered them in reverse order, and again, in both orders consecutively, so that he is able to lose himself in, as well as to emerge from, any one of

them, whenever he chooses, wherever he chooses, and for as long
as he chooses—when, too, by rooting out the Taints, he enters
into and abides in that emancipation of heart, that emancipation
of the intellect which he by himself, here in this present world,
has come to know and realise—then such a brother, Ānanda, is
called "Free-in-both-ways." And, Ānanda, any other Freedom-
in-both-ways higher and loftier than this Freedom-in-both-ways
there is not!' Rhys Davids. *Dialogues of the Buddha* Part II,
68-70 (*Mahā-Nidāna-Suttanta,* 35-6)

Cf also pages 118 and 173 in the same volume.

3.4.4 On letting the Tao circulate freely
The deluded man clings to the characteristics of things, adheres
to the *samadhi* of oneness, thinks that straightforward mind is
sitting without moving and casting aside delusions without
letting things arise in the mind. This he considers to be the
samadhi of oneness. This kind of practice is the same as in-
sentiency and the cause of an obstruction to the Tao. Tao must
be something that circulates freely; why should he impede it?
If the mind does not abide in things the Tao circulates freely;
if the mind abides in things it becomes entangled. Yampolsky.
The Platform Sutra of the Sixth Patriarch, 136

3.4.5 Suso's soul and the Divine Wisdom
It happened one morning that the Servitor saw in a vision that
he was surrounded by a troup of heavenly spirits. He therefore
asked one of the most radiant of these Princes of the Sky to show
him how God dwelt in his soul. The angel said to him, 'Do but
fix your eyes joyously upon yourself, and watch how God plays
the game of love within your loving soul.' And he looked
quickly, and saw that his body in the region of his heart was
pure and transparent like crystal : and he saw the Divine Wisdom peacefully enthroned in the midst of his heart, and she was
fair to look upon. And by her side was the soul of the Servitor,
full of heavenly desires; resting lovingly upon the bosom of

H

God, Who had embraced it and pressed it lovingly to His Heart. And it remained altogether absorbed and inebriated with love in the arms of God its well-beloved. Underhill. *Mysticism,* 343 (quoting M. Diepenbrock. *Heinrich Susos Leben und Schriften* (Regensburg 1825), cap.vi)

Suso lived in Germany, c. 1300-1365.

3.4.6   The meaning of 'I am God'

Take the famous utterance, 'I am God.' Some men reckon it as a great pretension; but 'I am God' is in fact a great humility. The man who says 'I am the servant of God' asserts that two exist, one himself and the other God. But he who says 'I am God' has naughted himself and cast himself to the winds. He says, 'I am God' : that is, 'I am not, He is all, nothing has existence but God, I am pure non-entity, I am nothing.' In this the humility is greater.

It is this that ordinary men do not understand. If a man renders a service *ad majorem Dei gloriam,* his servanthood is still present there; even though it is for the sake of God, he still sees himself and his own action as well as God; he is not drowned in the water. That man is drowned in the water, in whom no movement, no action remains, all his movements being the movement of the water.

A lion was chasing a deer, and the deer was fleeing from the lion. There were two beings in being, one that of the lion and the other that of the deer. But when the lion caught up with the deer and the deer, being overpowered beneath the lion's clutch, in terror of the lion became unconscious and senseless and collapsed before the lion, in that moment the being of the lion remained alone, the being of the deer was effaced and remained no more A. J. Arberry. *Discourses of Rūmī* (1961), 55-6

Jalāl al-Dīn Rūmī was a mystic and poet who lived in thirteenth century Persia.

3.5 POSSESSION, AUTOMATISM AND SPECIAL POWERS

States of mind which may be brought together loosely under these terms seem also to display links with all of the four preceding categories. For example, James marked out 'passivity' as being one of the keynotes of mystical states (perhaps inaccurately with respect to those in which no 'superior power' is supposed to play any part), and linked this passivity of will with involuntary action of different kinds such as prophetic speech, automatic writing and mediumistic trance (*The Varieties of Religious Experience*, 372). This merely serves to underline the need for an analysis at once more massively based and more precise. Cf 5.4.3 and 5.4.4.

3.5.1 The possession of Jeremiah

Now the word of the LORD came to me saying,
> 'Before I formed you in the womb I knew you,
> and before you were born I consecrated you;
> I appointed you a prophet to the nations.'

Then I said 'Ah, Lord GOD! Behold I do not know how to speak, for I am only a youth.' But the LORD said to me,
> 'Do not say, "I am only a youth";
> for to all to whom I send you you shall go,
> and whatever I command you you shall speak.
> Be not afraid of them,
> for I am with you to deliver you,' says the LORD.

Then the LORD put forth his hand and touched my mouth; and the LORD said to me,
> 'Behold, I have put my words in your mouth.
> See, I have set you this day over nations and over kingdoms,
> to pluck up and to break down,
> to destroy and to overthrow,
> to build and to plant.'

And the word of the LORD came to me, saying, 'Jeremiah,

what do you see?' And I said, 'I see a rod of almond [*shaqed*].' Then the LORD said to me, 'You have seen well, for I am watching [*shoqed*] over my word to perform it.'

Jeremiah i, 4-12.

3.5.2 Conversion with physical seizure

As the choir began to sing I felt a queer feeling about my heart, which might be called a nervous tremor. There was a choking sensation in my throat, and every muscle in my body seemed to have received an electric shock. While in this state, hardly knowing what I did, I went forward. On the second night I was converted, and felt that God was pleased with me. Starbuck. *The Psychology of Religion*, 79

One of Starbuck's cases.

3.5.3 Automatic writing (i)

Art has not wrote here, neither was there any time to consider how to set it punctually down, according to the Understanding of the Letters, but all was ordered according to the Direction of the Spirit, which often went in haste, so that in many words Letters may be wanting, and in some places a Capital Letter for a Word; so that the Penman's Hand, by reason he was not accustomed to it, did often shake. And though I could have wrote in a more accurate, fair and plain Manner, yet the Reason was this, that the burning Fire often forced forward with Speed, and the Hand and Pen must hasten directly after it; for it comes and goes as a sudden Shower. Underhill. *Mysticism*, 355-6 (quoting *The Works of Jacob Boehme*, English translation (1764-81), vol i, xiv)

3.5.4 Automatic writing (ii)

Moreover, writing the book of Ofudesaki, the Foundress informed people of the will of God the Parent and urged them to perform the service.

God the Parent urged 'Pen, pen, take up your pen.' She took up Her pen and the pen speedily moved even in the dark of the night as if it would in the daylight and the will of God the Parent was written down. When all was written down, the pen stopped short.

Thus She wrote the book of Ofudesaki, which is composed of seventeen parts and contains 1711 pieces of poetry. Tenrikyo Kyokai Honbu (ie Tenrikyo Church Head Office). *A Short History of Tenrikyo* (Tenri 1967), 81

3.5.5 Two modes of supernatural power

Moreover, lord, unsurpassable is the way in which the Exalted One teaches the Norm concerning modes of supernormal power, that there are two modes, to wit: (1) Supernormal power which is concomitant with the mental intoxicants and with worldly aims. This is called ignoble [power]. (2) Supernormal power which is not so concomitant. This is called noble [power]. And what, lord, is the former, the ignoble supernormal power? When, lord, some recluse or brahmin, by the means aforesaid, reaches up to such rapture of mind, that rapt in thought he becomes able to enjoy divers modes of supernormal power—from being one he becomes multiform, from being multiform he becomes one; from being visible he becomes invisible; he passes without hindrance to the further side of a wall, or a battelement, or a mountain, as if through air; he penetrates up and down through solid ground as if through water; he walks on water without dividing it as if on solid ground; he travels cross-legged through the sky, like a bird on the wing; he touches and feels with the hand even the moon and the sun, of mystic power and potency though they be; he reaches even in the body up to the heaven of Brahmā. This, lord, is the supernormal power, concomitant with the mental Intoxicants and with worldly aims, that is called ignoble. And what, lord, is the second mode, called noble? This is when a bhikkhu can, if he so desire, remain unconscious of disgust amid what is disgusting; or conscious of disgust amid what is not disgusting; or unconscious of disgust amid what is both disgusting and the opposite; or conscious of disgust amid what is both disgusting and the opposite; or, avoiding both that which is disgusting and the opposite, should remain indifferent to them as such, mindful and understanding. Rhys Davids. *Dialogues of the Buddha* Part III, 106-7 (*Sampasādaniya Suttanta*, 18)

PART FOUR

Religious Concepts

The conceptual side of religion is perhaps the most obvious aspect of the whole religious datum, and at the same time it provides us with countless millions of words of source material. What the religions of the world have to *say* about the world, human existence and their own role, might seem to be a major question in the comparative study of religion. Nevertheless it is a question which is not directly answered here, for two reasons. Firstly it has naturally proved impossible to treat the topics of the *other* sections without using source material of a verbal character, and so all of these contribute to a wider picture of religious ideas than could have been achieved in one short section alone. Secondly it seemed desirable to illustrate some of the ways in which religious concepts are comparable regardless of the variety or similarity of specific content. It will perhaps be readily agreed that 'myths', for example, are a widely comparable type of religious thinking, even though in terms of specific content *all myths are different*. By following up this slightly indirect approach a variety of topics have been raised which together indicate in an introductory way what sort of things religious concepts are and how they work. A comparative approach along these lines shows that religious conceptual systems are indeed comparable in various ways even when the contents of belief are different.

4.1 FUNDAMENTAL IDEAS

It is difficult to avoid the impression that a religious tradition maintains its characteristic form at least partly because of a few deep-seated concepts in terms of which the whole system is elaborated. For example, the idea of the one, omnipotent yet gracious God, whose will for the ordering of human life was authoritatively revealed in the Koran through the Prophet, is sufficient to have guaranteed the persistent unity of Islam in spite of a fantastic elaboration of detail in interpretation and adaptation to diverse cultures. Similarly the monistic polytheism of Hinduism can cope with any new variety of *form* in religion which does not compete with its basic principle. Or one might note the long history and insistent influence of the Iranian dualism of light and darkness, good and evil. For this reason an elementary classification of religious ideas by means of terms such as polytheism, nondualism, dualism, monotheism, henotheism, pantheism, and so on, is not without its point. However the definition of just what is precisely the central, controlling cluster of ideas is not always easy, especially as different representatives of one tradition may have very different interpretations to offer, or perhaps because different representatives may have very similar interpretations which differ slightly yet significantly. Moreover the central cluster of concepts is not simply to be expected to appear in terms of the various metaphysical options but must be perceived phenomenologically in terms of the total religious view of the believer (cf the use of the term 'focus' in Ninian Smart's *The Phenomenon of Religion,* 1972). Many extracts in this book, and especially those under 4.8, 4.9 and 4.10, may be considered in terms of this problem. The two adduced immediately below illustrate respectively the strength of such basic conceptions (often noted by anthropologists studying the ideas of *others*) and the introduction of a new controlling concept to an existing group.

4.1.1 The power of the nats

Educated in a Christian high school in Mandalay, my interpreter, for example, persistently denied that the nats could affect anyone's life, although he did not deny that they existed. When, however, he shared a house with my wife and me at the Taungbyon Festival, he asked us not to sleep together near the coconut which hangs for the house nat, lest we suffer some harm. Somewhat later, when visiting his house and noticing a suspended coconut, I asked him why he, a professed sceptic, observed this ritual. Embarrassed, he explained that because he recited his beads daily, he had no fear of the nats, but because his daughter did not recite her beads, it was necessary to hang the coconut, lest she be harmed by Min Mahagiri, the house nat. Melford E. Spiro. *Burmese Supernaturalism, A Study in the Explanation and Reduction of Suffering* (Englewood Cliffs 1967), 62

Nats are a whole range of supernatural beings having various locations and powers, widely believed in by the Burmese.

4.1.2 The identification of the Messiah

'Let me tell you plainly, my friends, that the patriarch David died and was buried, and his tomb is here to this very day. It is clear therefore that he spoke as a prophet who knew that God had sworn to him that one of his own direct descendants should sit on his throne; and when he said he was not abandoned to Hades, and his flesh never suffered corruption, he spoke with foreknowledge of the resurrection of the Messiah. The Jesus we speak of has been raised by God, as we can all bear witness. Exalted thus with God's right hand, he received the Holy Spirit from the Father, as was promised, and all that you now see and hear flows from him. For it was not David who went up to heaven; his own words are "The Lord said to my Lord, 'Sit at my right hand until I make your enemies your footstool.' "
Let all Israel then accept as certain that God has made this Jesus, whom you crucified, both Lord and Messiah.' Acts ii, 29-36

Christians and Jews shared the concept of one all-powerful God, acting historically and eschatologically through Israel in particular. The last two sentences above introduce the christological element distinctive of any Christian theology; and at the same time make an identification which subverts the wish for nationalist political victory.

4.2 MYTH

A myth is a more or less circumstantial tale with a cosmic setting, in terms of which those who use it are able to interpret their existence in the world. It is possible to subcategorise myths in terms of their subject-matter. For example there are myths of creation and origin, especially racial origin (cf below and 1.5.1, 6.2.1-2); myths of descent to the underworld, of pollution and purification (cf 1.3.2); dying and rising myths and myths of enthronement (of a deity); myths about the end of the world, judgement, new creation or utopia (cf 7.4.5); myths of cyclical repetition and infinite reduplication of worlds (cf 4.8.2, 7.1.1-2); myths of emanation and return, and so on. Myths may contain or may orginally have been based upon a variable degree of historical fact (cf the problem of categorisation referred to in 1.5). The contemporary interpretation of myths tends to take them very seriously as representing the needs and tensions of social and individual life in a variety of ways; this leads over into the plane of 'explanation' (cf especially 6.2 and 7.4). At the same time myths are closely associated with, if not quite inseparable from, the fundamental ideas of complex religions (cf especially 4.8.2 and 7.1). A separate volume would be required to give an elementary survey of mythological materials; but myth is an element found in numerous cases adduced here of which the cross-references given above represent a selection only.

4.2.1 Creation of land and divinities (i)

In one writing it is said: 'The two Deities were united and became husband and wife. First of all, the islands of Ahaji and Aha being considered the placenta, they produced the island of Oho-yamato no Toyo-aki-tsu-shima, next the island of Iyo, next the island of Tsukushi, next, as twins, the islands of Oki and Sado, next the island of Koshi, next Oho-shima, and next Kojima.' . . .

Now Izanami no Mikoto was burnt by Kagu tsuchi, so that she died. When she was lying down to die, she gave birth to the Earth-Goddess, Hani-yama-hime, and the Water-Goddess, Midzu-ha-no-me. Upon this Kagu tsuchi took to wife Hani-yama-hime, and they had a child named Waka-musubi. On the crown of this Deity's head were produced the silk-worm and the mulberry tree, and in her navel the five kinds of grain.

In one writing it is said: 'When Izanami no Mikoto gave birth to Ho-no-musubi, she was burnt by the child and died. When she was about to die, she brought forth the Water-Goddess, Midzu-ha-no-me, and the Earth-Goddess, Hani-yama-hime. She also brought forth the gourd of Heaven.'

In one writing it is said: 'When about to give birth to the Fire-God, Kagu tsuchi, Izanami no Mikoto became feverish and ill. In consequence she vomited, and the vomit became changed into a God, who was called Kana-yama-hiko. Next her urine became changed into a Goddess, who was called Midzu-ha-no-me. Next her excrement was changed into a Goddess, who was called Hani-yama-hime.

In one writing it is said: 'When Izanami no Mikoto gave birth to the Fire-God, she was burnt and died. She was, therefore, buried at the village of Arima in Kumano, in the province of Kii. In the time of flowers, the inhabitants worship the spirit of this Goddess by offerings of flowers. They also worship her with drums, flutes, flags, singing and dancing.' Aston. *Nihongi*, 17, 21-2

4.2.2   Creation of land and divinities (ii)

'The land standing there had as fish a gecko. But a woman brought in the animal and fed it as a pet. As time went on, her belly became great. Her folk invited all the people to come and discuss who was responsible for the pregnancy. They counted and counted heads until they were exhausted, but they did not fix precisely on her man. Then someone proposed to turn up the wooden bowl there, to see. When they turned it up, up jumped a man. The people murmured in astonishment at this. "Now, she had her man hidden indeed!" The man went down to the beach, dragged down his canoe, and voyaged away. But the woman arose, and went in her shame, went and dwelt on the nose tip or sandspit of the land. Then the land parted in two; one part stood firm while the tip of the land went with her. It went and stood, the land rose and made an encircling lowland. Its name was Rikoifenua . . .

'And a feast was prepared. They assembled and went to Rarokoka in Uta. When they came there Tikarau was sitting there. So they wrestled, and as they wrestled the Brethren were thrown. When they kept on being thrown, Rakiteua then went to Raropuka and unwound the belt of their mother, came back and he and Tikarau wrestled again. The body of the Atua i Tafua became hotter and hotter, but was cooled by the belt of his mother. As they continued, Tikarau fell. He crashed down, but ran off, gathered together all kinds of food, and disappeared. But as he was going he slipped down. The place of his falling is there at Marepa. As they ran after him the Atua i Tafua grabbed the coconut, then as he came to the yam, gave it to the Atua i Kafika, while the taro was grabbed by the Atua i Taumako, and Tafito grabbed the breadfruit. So the coconut obeys the Ariki Tafua in Tikopia here, the taro is under the control of the Ariki Taumako, the breadfruit is under the control of Tafito—people of this land go and crawl for fertility to sa Fangarere, that the breadfruit may bear. But the yam was allotted to the Atua i Kafika.' Raymond Firth, *History and Traditions of Tikopia* (Wellington 1961), 28-30

Firth's whole account and discussion of the varieties of Tikopian myth is very instructive.

4.3 LEGEND AND HAGIOGRAPHY

Religious legends deal with specific persons and events, often in a hagiographical vein. Some borderline cases may not be easily distinguishable from myth. The distinctive characteristics of religious legend seem to be a combination of the circumstantial and the miraculous, together with a more or less explicit indication of the religious meaning conveyed in the story.

4.3.1 The Buddha crosses the Ganges

But the Exalted One went on to the river. And at that time the river Ganges was brimful and overflowing; and wishing to cross to the opposite bank, some began to seek for boats, some for rafts of wood, whilst some made rafts of basket-work. Then the Exalted One as instantaneously as a strong man would stretch forth his arm, or draw it back again when he had stretched it forth, vanished from this side of the river, and stood on the further bank with the company of the brethren.

And the Exalted One beheld the people who wished to cross to the opposite bank looking some of them for boats and some of them for rafts of wood, and some of them for rafts of basket-work; and as he beheld them he broke forth at that time into this song :

'They who have crossed the ocean drear
Making a solid path across the pools—
Whilst the vain world ties its basket rafts—
These are the wise, these are the saved indeed!'

End of the First Portion for Recitation.

Rhys Davids *Dialogues of the Buddha* Part II, 94-5

The ocean is said to mean craving, the solid path is the Buddhist eightfold path and the rafts of the vain world are other, inadequate religious practices. Thus the legend is used as an allegory.

4.3.2   Jesus and the big haul of fish

When he [Jesus] had finished speaking, he said to Simon, 'Put out into deep water and let down your nets for a catch.' Simon answered, 'Master, we were hard at work all night and caught nothing at all; but if you say so, I will let down the nets.' They did so and made a big haul of fish ; and their nets began to split. So they signalled to their partners in the other boat to come and help them. This they did, and loaded both boats to the point of sinking. When Simon saw what had happened he fell at Jesus' knees and said, 'Go, Lord, leave me, sinner that I am!' For he and all his companions were amazed at the catch they had made; so too were his partners James and John, Zebedee's sons. 'Do not be afraid,' said Jesus to Simon! 'from now on you will be catching men.' As soon as they had brought the boats to land, they left everything and followed him. Luke v, 4-11

Although this legend is given by Luke as an incident in the ministry of Jesus, one has to appreciate the previous role it must also have played in the oral tradition of the early Church, sometimes in need, no doubt, of encouragement about the power of the *risen* Jesus. Cf John xxi, 4-13.

4.3.3   Thomas Aquinas is called to heaven

At Naples too God was pleased to make known the death of the Saint in a miraculous manner. One of the friars, whilst praying in the church, fell into an ecstasy, in which he seemed to behold the holy Doctor teaching in the schools, surrounded by a vast multitude of disciples. St Paul the Apostle then appeared, with a company of saints, and St Thomas asked him if he had interpreted his Epistles rightly. 'Yes,' replied the Apostle, 'as far as anyone still in the flesh can understand them; but come with me; I will lead you to a place where you will have a clearer understanding of all things.' The Apostle then seemed to lay his hand on St Thomas's mantle and to lead him away; and the friar who beheld the vision startled the community by crying out three times in a loud voice : 'Alas! alas! our Doctor is being taken away from us!' (Anonymous member of the Dominican Order.) *St Thomas Aquinas* (Catholic Truth Society 1948), 23

This legend contains a vision, not only of the departure of Thomas Aquinas, but also of the status of the efforts of the human intellect.

4.4 SYMBOLS AND SYSTEMS

Symbols and systems are usually concentrated and expanded representations respectively of a common matter. Thus the opening line of every *sūra* of the Koran but one, 'In the name of God, the merciful, the compassionate' is a concise exclamation of the Islamic faith otherwise expounded in variety and length. At the same time it binds together the Koranic revelation as a whole, and to it the daily life of every Muslim who repeats this line before eating or on other occasions. A similar claim could be made for the Sikh *Japjī,* which, though longer, is equally representative of the Granth as a whole. Christian creeds too have been traditionally known as 'symbols' of the faith, as for example in Rufinus' systematic *Commentarius in Symbolum Apostolorum* (circa AD 390).

Such symbols may be reduced to an almost purely visual form, as when a verse such as 'Muhammed is the messenger of God', or even a whole *sūra,* is written not in an extended line but as a symmetrical pattern, or as in the case of the 'seed-syllables' of Indian religions, or the calligraphic mandala of Nichiren which sums up the whole systematic tradition of Tendai Buddhism.

Space forbids dealing with the very interesting topic of the personification of abstract ideas from religious thought-systems. It is also quite impossible to deal comparatively here with systematic religious thought as such.

4.4.1   The syllable 'OM' and all the Vedas

The Supreme Being created Brahmā, the creator on the lotus.
Having been created, that Brahmā began to think, 'By which
single syllable may I be able to enjoy all the desires, all the
worlds, all the gods, all the Vedas, all the sacrifices, all the
sounds, all the rewards, all the beings, stationary and moving?'
He practised self-control and saw this OM, of two syllables . . .
the Brahman's own symbolic syllable, of which the pre-
siding divinity is Brahman itself. Morgan. *The Religion of
the Hindus* (New York 1953), 294 (*Gopatha Brahmana* I,
16ff)

The conception is widespread. Cf also especially *Chandogya
Upanishad* I, II and III.

4.4.2   Mantras

Japa is the repetition of a group of mystic syllables technically
called a *mantra*. A *mantra* is not a mere formula or a magic
spell or a prayer; it is an embodiment in sound of a particular
deity. It is the deity itself. And so, when a mantra is repeated a
hundred times, or a thousand times, or even more, and the worshipper makes an effort to identify himself with the worshipped,
the power of the deity comes to his help. Human power is thus
supplemented by the divine power. A prayer is different from
the repetition of a mantra, for it is a purely human effort. One
may pray in any language and in any form, but a mantra, being
an embodiment of a deity in sound, has to be repeated in that
form alone in which it first revealed itself to the mind of a Seer,
a Rishi. It is not to be learned from books, but from the living
voice of a teacher, a *guru,* who gives the initiation, and it has for
its object the gradual transformation of the personality of the
worshipper into that of the worshipped. D. S. Sarma. 'The
Nature and History of Hinduism', in Morgan. *The Religion of
the Hindus,* 24-5

The writer of the above is a modern exponent of Hinduism.

4.4.3 Why systematic buddhology is necessary

Question : What need is there to repeat the explanation of the teaching when it is presented in detail in the sutras?

Answer : Though this teaching is presented in the sutras, the capacity and the deeds of men today are no longer the same, nor are the conditions of their acceptance and comprehension. That is to say, in the days when the Tathāgata was in the world, people were of high aptitude and the Preacher excelled in his form, mind, and deeds, so that once he had preached with his perfect voice, different types of people all equally understood; hence, there was no need for this kind of discourse. But after the passing away of the Tathāgata, there were some who were able by their own power to listen extensively to others and to reach understanding; there were some who by their own power could listen to very little and yet understand much; there were some who, without any mental power of their own, depended upon the extensive discourses of others to obtain understanding; and naturally there were some who looked upon the wordiness of extensive discourses as troublesome, and who sought after what was comprehensive, terse, and yet contained much meaning, and then were able to understand it. Thus, this discourse is designed to embrace, in a general way, the limitless meaning of the vast and profound teaching of the Tathāgata. This discourse, therefore, should be presented. Yoshihito S. Hakeda (trans). *The Awakening of Faith* (New York 1967), 26-7

The teaching of the Buddha could be expressed either in 'extended' sutras or in very brief ones, or even, according to some, in mantra form. The writer of this very influential sixth century Chinese treatise (piously ascribed to Aśvaghosha) emphasises that the length of a systematic buddhology should be appropriate to its reader.

4.4.4 The Holy Trinity and the sign of the cross

The doctrine of the Holy Trinity is a brief compendium of the teachings of Christianity. Hence, in professing our belief in this

I

mystery, we at the same time proclaim our faith in all the doctrines of our holy religion. We further begin our prayers, labours,
etc, with the sign of the cross, saying : 'In the name of the
Father,' etc. This is equivalent to a solemn declaration that we
intend to undertake and perform all things in the name, and in
obedience to the Tri-une God, and that from him we expect
blessing and success for all our undertakings . . .

By the sign of the cross we express the wish and prayer that,
through the merits of the crucified Saviour, we may be preserved
from all evils of soul and body, and that, in view of the death
of Jesus Christ upon the cross, our daily labours and our various
occupations may prosper and become meritorious in the
sight of God. Shadler. *The Beauties of the Catholic Church,*
100-1

4.4.5   The Ave Maria of Thomas Aquinas
The angelic doctor was full of childlike devotion to our Blessed
Lady. His confessor, Brother Reginald, declared that St Thomas
had never asked anything through Mary without obtaining it;
and the Saint himself specially attributed to her intercession the
grace of living and dying in the Dominican Order, according
to his own earnest desire. During the whole of one Lent he
preached on the words 'Ave Maria', and the same cherished
words are to be found in his own handwriting over and over
again on the margin of an autograph copy of the 'Summa
against the Gentiles', recently discovered in Italy. (Anonymous
member of the Dominican Order). *St Thomas Aquinas* (Catholic
Truth Society 1948), 19-20

Whether this legend is true or not may be left unasked, but note
the juxtaposition of the repeated 'Ave Maria' which speaks
volumes and the 'Summa' which *is* volumes.

_____

4.5   CRUDITY AND SUBTLETY IN RELIGIOUS
LANGUAGE
The very rich use of simile and metaphor in religion is suffi-

cient to account for some curious parallels (4.5.1, 2 and 3). As an example of widespread comparability, not illustrated below, we may note the use of human relationships as metaphors for religious relationships.

The fact that religious language is dependent on ordinary language and subject to its limitations, while at the same time having special reference, has been widely recognised by mystical and religious writers of all times. The early allegorical method of exegesis, the medieval doctrine of analogy and the modern debate over demythologisation are a sufficient indication of this, to take the systematic side of the Christian tradition alone. To a greater or lesser extent there has *always* been tension between the more literal and the more subtle approach to religious meanings. Sometimes the same basic idea is understood in different ways (4.5.4, 5 and 6). Sometimes, again, sheer baffle about the status of a traditional concept is deliberately provoked (4.5.7 and 8). Cf 7.1

4.5.1 Failure of the rootless (i)

It is the same with those who receive the seed on rocky ground; as soon as they hear the word, they accept it with joy, but it strikes no root in them; they have no staying-power; then, when there is trouble or persecution on account of the word, they fall away at once. Mark iv, 16-17

4.5.2 Failure of the rootless (ii)

When people of shallow capacity hear the Sudden Doctrine being preached they are like the naturally shallow-rooted plants on this earth, which, after a deluge of rain, are all beaten down and cannot continue their growth. Yampolsky. *The Platform Sutra of the Sixth Patriarch* 150

4.5.3 Failure of the rootless (iii)

Some people have read a few Marxist books and think themselves quite learned, but what they have read has not penetrated, has not struck root in their minds, so that they do not know how to use it and their class feelings remain as of old. Others are very conceited and having learned some book-phrases, think themselves terrific and are very cocky; but whenever a storm blows up, they take a stand very different from that of the workers and the majority of the peasants. They waver while the latter stand firm, they equivocate while the latter are forthright. Mao Tse-tung. *Quotations from Chairman Mao Tse-tung* (Peking 1966), 311

4.5.4　The resurrection body (Baruch)

'Nevertheless, I will again ask from Thee, O Mighty One, yea, I will ask mercy from Him who made all things.

" In what shape will those live who live in Thy day?

Oh how will the splendour of those who (are) after that time continue?

Will they then resume this form of the present,

And put on these entrammelling members,

Which are now involved in evils,

And in which evils are consummated,

Or wilt Thou perchance change these things which have been in the world

As also the world?" '

And He answered and said unto me: 'Hear, Baruch, this word,

And write in the remembrance of thy heart all that thou shalt learn.

For the earth shall then assuredly restore the dead,

[Which it now receives, in order to preserve them].

It shall make no change in their form,

But as it has received, so shall it restore them,

And as I delivered them unto it, so also shall it raise them.

For then it will be necessary to show to the living that the dead have come to life again, and that those who had departed have returned (again). R. H. Charles. *The Apocrypha and*

Pseudepigrapha of the Old Testament in English (Oxford 1913), 508 (*The Apocalypse of Baruch* 49-50)

This represents a late first-century Jewish view of the resurrection of the dead. Cf next extract.

4.5.5 The resurrection body (Paul)

But, you may ask, how are the dead raised? In what kind of body? A senseless question! The seed you sow does not come to life unless it has first died; and what you sow is not the body that shall be, but a naked grain, perhaps of wheat, or of some other kind; and God clothes it with the body of his choice, each seed with its own particular body. All flesh is not the same flesh : there is flesh of men, flesh of beasts, of birds, and of fishes—all different. There are heavenly bodies and earthly bodies; and the splendour of the heavenly bodies is one thing, the splendour of the earthly, another. The sun has a splendour of its own, the moon another splendour, and the stars another, for star differs from star in brightness. So it is with the resurrection of the dead. What is sown in the earth as a perishable thing is raised imperishable. Sown in humiliation, it is raised in glory; sown in weakness, it is raised in power; sown as an animal body, it is raised as a spiritual body. 1 Corinthians xv, 35-44

Paul attempted here to cope with disbelief in the general resurrection of the dead. This was not a point of Jewish-Christian controversy, and there seem to have been Christians who presented the matter rather as it appears in the previous extract (4.5.4) and again others who found it difficult to accept in those terms. Paul's writing predates the *Apocalypse of Baruch* but ideas found in the latter are presumed to have been current for some time.

4.5.6 The resurrection body (Athenagoras)

. . . and there must be some appropriate end proposed for this life. But if it is the end of both parts together, and this can be discovered neither while they are still living in the present state of existence through the numerous causes already mentioned, nor yet when the soul is in a state of separation, because the man cannot be said to exist when the body is dissolved, and indeed entirely scattered abroad, even though the soul continue by itself—it is absolutely necessary that the end of man's being should appear in some reconstitution of the two together, and of the same living being. And as this follows of necessity, there must by all means be a resurrection of the bodies which are dead, or even entirely dissolved, and the same men must be formed anew, since the law of nature ordains the end not absolutely, nor as the end of any men whatsoever, but of the same men who passed through the previous life; but it is impossible for the same men to be reconstituted unless the same bodies are restored to the same souls. But that the same soul should obtain the same body is impossible in any other way, and possible only by the resurrection; for if this take place, an end befitting the nature of men follows also. Dods, Reith and Pratten (trans). *The Writings of Justin Martyr and Athenagoras* (Edinburgh 1867), 455-6 (*On the Resurrection* XXV)

Athenagoras was a Christian apologist writing towards the end of the second century. Cf the preceding extracts.

4.5.7 The meaning of 'authority'

And as he [Jesus] was walking in the temple court the chief priests, lawyers, and elders came to him and said, 'By what authority are you acting like this? Who gave you authority to act in this way?' Jesus said to them, 'I will ask you one question; and if you give me an answer, I will tell you by what authority I act. The baptism of John: was it from God, or from men? Answer me.' This set them arguing among themselves: 'What shall we say? If we say, "from God," he will say, "Then why did you not believe him?" Shall we say, "from men"?'—but they were afraid of the people, for all held that John was in fact a prophet. So they answered Jesus, 'We do not know.' And

Jesus said to them, 'Then neither will I tell you by what authority I act.' Mark xi, 27-33

4.5.8 The meaning of 'zazen'
A monk asked Seijō of Kōyō and said, 'Daitsū Chishō Buddha did zazen for ten aeons in a Meditation Hall, and could neither manifest the truth, nor enter the Buddha-way. Why was this?' Seijō said, 'Your question is a very appropriate one.' The monk persisted, 'Why did he not attain Buddhahood by doing zazen in the Meditation Hall?' Seijō replied, 'Because he didn't.' R. H. Blyth. *Zen and Zen Classics* (Tokyo 1966), 90

This passage is 'Case IX' of the *Mumonkan,* a thirteenth centurny Chinese work translated in the above volume. *Zazen* means literally 'sitting meditation'.

4.6 CREATING RELIGIOUS CONCEPTS
It is interesting to notice the varying degrees of self-consciousness on the part of those responsible for the creation or development of religious concepts. Writers of systematic works tend to have clear-cut intentions which are often deliberately stated (cf 4.4.3). Elsewhere however there is a much more confused area, in which the role of the creative religious specialist and the purpose of the concepts are hinted at, yet at the same time concealed under the religious motifs themselves.

4.6.1 Finding the book of the law
And Hilkiah the high priest said to Shaphan the secretary, 'I have found the book of the law in the house of the Lord.' And Hilkiah gave the book to Shaphan, and he read it . . . Then Shaphan the secretary told the king, 'Hilkiah the priest has given me a book.' And Shaphan read it before the king.

And when the king heard the words of the book of the law,

he rent his clothes. And the king commanded Hilkiah the priest, and Ahikam the son of Shaphan, and Achbor the son of Micaiah, and Shaphan the secretary, and Asaiah the king's servant, saying, 'Go, inquire of the Lord for me, and for the people, and for all Judah, concerning the words of this book that has been found; for great is the wrath of the Lord that is kindled against us, because our fathers have not obeyed the words of this book, to do according to all that is written concerning us . . .

And the king went up to the house of the Lord, and with him all the men of Judah and all the inhabitants of Jerusalem, and the priests and the prophets, all the people both small and great; and he read in their hearing all the words of the book of the covenant which had been found in the house of the Lord. And the king stood by the pillar and made a covenant before the Lord, to walk after the Lord and to keep his commandments and his testimonies and his statutes, with all his heart and all his soul, to perform the words of this covenant that were written in this book; and all the people joined in the covenant. 2 Kings xxii, 8, 10, 11-13; xxiii, 2, 3

The 'finding' of this book was the starting-point of the 'Deuteronomic reform' under King Josiah of Judah in 621 BC.

4.6.2 The revealing of the Koran

> Even so We have sent it down
> as an Arabic Koran, and We
> have turned about in it something
> of threats, that haply they may be
> godfearing, or it may arouse in
>   them remembrance.
> So high exalted be God, the true King!
> And hasten not with the Koran ere
> its revelation is accomplished unto
> thee; and say, 'O my Lord, increase
>   me in knowledge.'

Arthur J. Arberry. *The Koran Interpreted* (1955), Vol 1, 347 (sura xx, 112-13)

4.6.3 The devotion to the Sacred Heart

In 1675 there lived in the convent of the Visitation at Paray-le-Monial, in France, a pious nun named Margaret Mary Alacoque. Practising the most exact obedience, she renounced entirely her own will, and embraced that of God alone as manifested to her by her superiors. Her love for God was equalled only by her contempt for herself and for all that was of the world. It was this soul, so pure, that God made choice of to establish the devotion to the Sacred Heart, and in the following manner: One day, during the octave of Corpus Christi, whilst she was engaged in prayer before the Blessed Sacrament, Jesus Christ, her Beloved, suddenly appeared before her, and, uncovering his breast, showed her his Heart. This Divine Heart, enthroned, as it were, in flames, was surrounded by a crown of thorns, and the wound it had received was still open, while a cross, more brilliant than the sun, surmounted all. After permitting his servant to contemplate this spectacle for a time in silence, our Lord uttered these loving words: 'Behold this Heart, which so loves men as to spare itself in nothing, even exhausting itself and being consumed for the love of them. Yet, in return, I receive from the greater number only ingratitude, through the coldness and contempt they exhibit for me in the Sacrament of my love, or through the irreverences and sacrileges of which they are guilty; and what wounds me more than all else is, that I am thus treated by hearts that are consecrated to me. It is my desire, therefore, that the first Friday after the octave of the Blessed Sacrament be observed in a special manner as the feast of my Heart, by offering a Communion, with a reparation of honour for all the insults and indignities which it has received since the institution of the Sacrament of the Altar. I promise that my Heart shall bestow its love abundantly on those who will render me this honour, or cause the same to be rendered me by others.' Shadler. *The Beauties of the Catholic Church*, 140-1

4.6.4   George Fox sees the nature of evil

And I went back into Nottinghamshire, and there the Lord shewed me that the natures of those things, which were hurtful without, were within the hearts and minds of wicked men. The natures of dogs, swine, vipers, of Sodom and Egypt, Pharaoh, Cain, Ishmael, Esau, etc, the natures of these I saw within, though people had been looking without. And I cried to the Lord, saying, 'Why should I be thus, seeing I was never addicted to commit those evils?' And the Lord answered, that it was needful I should have a sense of all conditions : how else should I speak to all conditions? And in this I saw the infinite love of God. *Christian Life Faith and Thought in the Society of Friends* (1922), 17

4.6.5   Gotama names the hells

Thus when the elder Mahā-Maudgalyāyana had seen the beings in the eight hells undergoing their thousands of torments he came to the four assemblies in the Jeta Grove and recounted it all at length. 'Thus,' said he, 'do the beings in the eight great hells and the sixteen secondary hells endure thousands of different torments. Therefore, one must strive after knowledge, win it, be enlightened, be fully enlightened, do good, and live the holy life. And in this world no sinful act must be committed.' . . .

Gotama, the Exalted One, the seer with clear insight into all things, has in his understanding named the eight hells, Sañjīva, Kālasūtra, Sanghāta, the two Rauravas, Mahāvīci, Tapana and Prₐtāpana.

Thus are these eight hells named. Hard are they to traverse, being strewn with the consequences of terrible deeds. Jones, *The Mahāvastu* Vol 1 (1949), 9

The Mahāvastu is a massive elaboration of Buddhist legend and myth, in which the various hells are described in detail. There is no escape from these hells until all effects of bad karma are exhausted, but the naming and describing of them has a good purpose.

4.6.6 The Buddhas as teachers

'Hear from me, son of Sari, how this Dharma has been fully known by the best of men, and how the enlightened leaders teach it through many hundreds of skilful means. Of innumerable living beings, so varied in their inclinations, I know the dispositions and conduct, for I have a knowledge of the various deeds they have done in the past, and of the merit they then acquired. With manifold explanations and reasonings I cause these beings to reach a greater spirituality; with hundreds of arguments and illustrations I gratify all beings, some in this way, some in that. At one time I have taught them the nine-fold Scripture, which is composed of the "Sutras", the "Verses", the section called "Thus was it said", the "Birth-stories", the "Marvels", the "Origins", the sections consisting of mingled prose and verse, the "Expositions", and hundreds of Similes in addition. Therein I exhibit Nirvana to those kinds of people who are content with inferior things, who are relatively ignorant, who have not for very long practised under the Buddhas of the past, and who have got stuck in the Samsaric world and suffer greatly from it. This is really only a skilful device by which the Self-Existent wishes to prepare them for the day when he can awake them to the cognition of a Buddha.' E. Conze, *Buddhist Scriptures* (Harmondsworth 1959), 200

This passage is from the Lotus Sutra, an early Mahayana Buddhist work.

4.6.7 Revolutionary culture

Revolutionary culture is a powerful revolutionary weapon for the broad masses of the people. It prepares the ground ideologically before the revolution comes and is an important, indeed essential, fighting front in the general revolutionary front during the revolution. Mao Tse-tung. *Quotations from Chairman Mao Tse-tung* (Peking 1966), 299-30

4.7   AUTHORITY AND TRADITION

Concepts of authority and tradition have tended to be very similar in religions which are otherwise quite different as to their doctrine. It is not surprising that such concepts usually involve reference to specially competent persons, singly or corporately, and to writings certified as authoritative. These may be linked in various ways with the central teachings of the religions concerned. Conversely debates about the meaning of a religion frequently include a debate about what counts as authoritative and what the precise shape of the religious tradition is which is supposed to be interpreted. As such debate proceeds authoritative writings may be gradually expanded, and they may also be treated with severe selectivity.

4.7.1   Tradition in Zen Buddhism

'At midnight the Fifth Patriarch called me into the hall and expounded the Diamond Sutra to me. Hearing it but once, I was immediately awakened, and that night I received the Dharma. None of the others knew anything about it. Then he transmitted to me the Dharma of Sudden Enlightenment and the robe, saying: "I make you the Sixth Patriarch. The robe is the proof and is to be handed down from generation to generation. My Dharma must be transmitted from mind to mind. You must make people awaken to themselves."

'The Fifth Patriarch told me: "From ancient times the transmission of the Dharma has been as tenuous as a dangling thread. If you stay here there are people who will harm you. You must leave at once" . . . The Master said: "The first transmission was from the Seven Buddhas [of the past], and Śākyamuni was the seventh. Eighth was Kāśyapa, ninth Ānanda, tenth Madhyāntika . . . thirty-fourth Śubhamitra, thirty-fifth Bodhidharma, prince from southern India, thirty-sixth, the Chinese priest Hui-k'o, thirty-seventh Seng-ts'an, thirty-eighth Tao-hsin, thirty-ninth Hung-jen, and as of now I am the fortieth to have received the Law."

'The Master said: "From today on transmit the teaching among yourselves, but be sure that you have the sanction, and do not let the essentials of the teaching become lost".' Yampolsky. *The Platform Sutra of the Sixth Patriarch*, 133, 179

Dharma, ie the teaching. The idea of a series of Buddhas arose early in the history of Buddhist thought. This attempt to link the Zen Patriarchs with the disciples of Śākyamuni is quite artifical with regard to detail.

4.7.2 Bishops in early Christianity

See that you all follow the bishop, as Jesus Christ follows the Father, and follow the presbytery as you would the apostles: and respect the deacons as you respect God's commandment. Let no one do any of the things pertaining to the church without the bishop. Let that be considered a valid eucharist which is held under the bishop or someone to whom he has entrusted it. Wherever the bishop appears, let the people be; just as wherever Jesus Christ is, the catholic church is . . . Kirsopp Lake (ed and trans). *The Apostolic Fathers*. The Loeb Classical Library (1965), 261 (Ignatius, *To the Smyrnaeans* VIII) (slightly adapted)

Written very early in the 2nd century AD.

4.7.3 Scripture and tradition

The Holy, Oecumenical and General Synod of Trent . . . having this aim always before its eyes, that errors may be removed and the purity of the Gospel be preserved in the Church, which was before promised through the prophets in the Holy Scriptures and which our Lord Jesus Christ the Son of God first published by his own mouth and then commanded to be preached through his Apostles to every creature as a source of all saving truth and of discipline of conduct; and perceiving that this truth and this discipline are contained in written books and in unwritten traditions, which were received by the Apostles from the lips of Christ himself, or, by the same Apostles, at the dictation of the Holy Spirit, and were handed on and have come down to us; following the example of the orthodox Fathers, this Synod receives and venerates, with equal pious affection and reverence, all the books both of the New and the Old Testaments, since one God is the author of both, together with the said Traditions, as well those pertaining to faith as those pertaining to morals, as having been given either from the lips of Christ or by the dictation of the Holy Spirit and preserved by unbroken succession in the Catholic Church . . . Henry Bettenson. *Documents of the Christian Church* (1943), 365 (quoting H. Denzinger. *Enchiridion Symbolorum, definitionum et declarationum etc.* (Freiburg 1922), 783)

This view of the relation between scripture and tradition was defined at the Council of Trent (first session 1545-8) in opposition to the protestant appeal to scripture alone.

4.7.4   Guru Granth in an Indian village

It is believed that the tenth Guru nominated the Granth as his successor and it is called Guru Granth by the Sikhs. It contains mainly the writings of the first five Gurus and a verse of the ninth Guru as well as the writings of some Muslim saints like Kabir and Farid and Hindu bhagats like Namdev, Dhanna and Surdas. Most of the Daleke villagers believe that the Granth has life and feels the heat of summer and the cold of winter like any other living person. It is wrapped in cotton clothes in summer and in warm clothes in winter. Some persons were seen fanning the Granth in summer. Utmost respect is paid to it by all. Nobody will touch the book unless he has taken a bath and washed himself, and no one sits bareheaded or with shoes on before it . . . Some persons were seen in Daleke and Taran Taran pressing the legs of the cot on which the Granth had been opened. This is similar to pressing the legs of guests, Rajas and Kings as a matter of respect. The Sikhs refer to their Guru as King of Kings. That this practice is widespread among Sikhs is evident from the fact that the instructions issued by the Sikh Ceremonies and Customs sub-committee of the Shiromani Gurdwara Prabhandak Committee has made a special mention of it and has asked Sikhs not to continue such practices which were Unsikh-like. Indera P. Singh. 'Religion in Daleke, a Sikh Village', in Viyarthi. *Aspects of Religion in Indian Society*, 209-11

4.8 REINTERPRETATIONS

Religious traditions are frequently reinterpreted. This happens especially when believers come to find aspects of received doctrine incomprehensible, incredible or irrelevant, when new circumstances arise which require to be understood in terms of an existing religious tradition, or when new religions are founded incorporating existing materials. Such reinterpretations are often naturally linked with questions about what is the 'real meaning' or 'essence' of the tradition in question, and about what is 'orthodox' and what is 'heretical'.

4.8.1 The story of Joseph in the Koran

And when they came in before Joseph, he took his parents unto him, and said : 'Come into Egypt safe, if Allah will !'

And he placed his parents on the dais and they fell down before him prostrate, and he said : 'Oh my father! This is the interpretation of my dream of old. My Lord hath made it true, and He hath shown me kindness, since he took me out of the prison and hath brought you from the desert after Satan had made strife between me and my brethren. Lo! my Lord is tender unto whom He will. He is the Knower, the Wise.

'Oh my Lord! Thou hast given me [something] of sovereignty and hast taught me [something] of the interpretation of events —Creator of the heavens and the earth! Thou art my Protecting Friend in the world and the Hereafter. Make me to die submissive (unto Thee), and join me to the righteous Mohammed

Marmaduke Pickthall. *The Meaning of the Glorious Koran* (New York, no date) 181 (*sūrah* xii, 99-101)

The whole of Sura 12 may be compared with Genesis xxxvii-xlviii and the above passage especially with Genesis xlvi, 28ff. Note the emphasis here on the sovereign graciousness of God, and on submission to him on the part of the righteous.

4.8.2 The real meaning of the 'Pure Land'

The prefect bowed deeply and asked : 'I notice that some monks and laymen always invoke the Buddha Amitābha and desire to be reborn in the West. I beg of you to explain whether one can be born there or not, and thus resolve my doubts.'

The Master said : 'Prefect, listen and I shall explain things for you. At Śrāvastī the World-honoured One preached of the Western Land in order to convert people, and it is clearly stated in the sutra, "[The Western Land] is not far." It was only for the sake of people of inferior capacity that the Buddha spoke of farness; to speak of nearness is only for those of superior attainments. Although in man there are naturally two types, in the Dharma there is no inequality. In delusion and awakening there is a difference, as may be seen in slowness and fastness of understanding. The deluded person concentrates on Buddha and wishes to be born in the other land; the awakened person makes pure his own mind . . . Perfect, practice only the ten virtues. Why should you seek rebirth [in the Western Land]? If you do not cut off the ten evils, what Buddha can you ask to come to welcome you? If you awaken to the sudden Dharma of birthlessness, you will see the Western Land in an instant. If you do not awaken to the Sudden Teaching of Mahāyāna, even if you concentrate on the Buddha and seek to be reborn, the road will be long. How can you hope to reach there?' Yampolsky. *The Platform Sutra of the Sixth Patriarch*, 156-8

The 'Western Land' is a mythical Buddha-land in which faithful devotees of Amitābha can be reborn as a preliminary to attaining Nirvana. This demythologisation by Hui-neng, the legendary founder of the southern school of Ch'an (Zen) in eighth century China, is arguably though not self-evidently consistent with the original intention of the mythology in Indian Buddhism. At the same time it is used here to emphasise the 'suddenness' of enlightenment, a point of contention in the time of Hui-neng.

4.8.3 The role of intellectuals in Marxism

Since the 'September strikes' (Federal Republic of Germany and Belgium) the student left has reconsidered its attitude towards the working class. A discussion is thereby reopened which is as old as Marxism itself : what role do 'intellectuals' play in the class struggle? Contemporary positions fluctuate between two extremes.

The traditional account is that in terms of origin and behaviour intellectuals belong to the 'petit bourgeois' class which aligns itself politically with the upper middle class, upon which it is economically dependent. Within the petite bourgeoisie the intellectuals display a wavering, opportunist attitude as between the bourgeoisie and the working class. Socialist oriented intellectuals must therefore leave their own class and subordinate themselves to the proletariat. The other extreme account is that as a consequence of the 'technological revolution' the 'technological intellectuals' have become a class of their own. This is because they bring their scientific and organisational work into the industrial process as a 'new productive strength' and because in their own way they are exploited just as the 'classical' proletariat is . . . It was not only the new activities of the working class which stimulated this discussion but also the students' own experiences in higher education. During the 'antiauthoritarian phase' the struggle at the place of work, the universities, was against authoritative and dogmatic methods and against state direction of the sciences. But the struggle soon brought an ally who was hardly expected and certainly undesired, namely industry, which also objects to non-rational education but with

K

quite a different purpose which is that it expects more 'efficiency' from further education . . . In order to develop a new approach in this situation something is being taken up which was previously neglected, namely the 'systematic study of the classical writers of Marxism'. Together with the classics the problem about the relationship between 'being and consciousness' is being newly posed. What, after all, is 'intelligence'? Polemos. 'Die Rolle der Intelligenz' (editorial), *Polemos* Heft 14 (Basel October 1970)

'Classical writers of Marxism' is a precise concept referring to Marx, Engels and Lenin, and an argument is not normally accepted as valid in Marxist groups unless it can be substantiated by reference to these classics. In his work *Ludwig Feuerbach und der Ausgang der klassischen deutschen Philosophie* (1888), Engels described the problem about the relationship between being and thought as the fundamental problem of philosophy.

4.9 SYNCRETISMS

Syncretism is the coherent yet somewhat uneasy coexistence of elements drawn from diverse religious contexts. Even when a smooth cohesion has been achieved the various elements often seem to maintain their potential for conveying independent meanings. If all trace of ambiguity disappears it becomes possible to speak of assimilation rather than syncretism, and this may be appropriate in the last case brought below—though one never knows.

4.9.1 Heroics and providence in Beowulf

Still resolute, and bearing his reputation in mind, Beowulf did not in the least lose heart. Exasperated, the hero flung down the patterned sword so that it fell stiff and sharp upon the ground. He trusted to his strength and to the might of his hands. This is how a man who hopes to win lasting fame on the field of battle should behave, and not care for his life. The Geat prince did not hesitate, but seized Grendel's mother by the shoulder. In his rage he flung his antagonist crashing to the floor. But she immediately came back at him with a ferocious grapple, closing in till the hero, who was strongest of fighting-men, weakened, stumbled, and took a fall. Then she threw herself on her visitor, unsheathing her broad bright-bladed dagger to avenge her only child. The woven chainmail about his shoulders saved his life by denying entrance to point and edge. Yet the son of Ecgtheow, champion of the Geats, would have perished deep underground if that chainmail corselet had not helped him. For God brought about the victory. Once Beowulf had struggled to his feet, the holy and omniscient ruler of the sky easily settled the issue in favour of the right. David Wright (trans). *Beowulf* (Harmondsworth 1957), 63

4.9.2 Self-expression and the Gospel

In his spontaneous and unrestricted imaginative work of painting, drawing and craft, the child will find the form of expression appropriate to him as a reply to the Gospel he has heard . . . This whole approach to religious instruction is often questioned. Is it really appropriate to its purpose? Surely religious instruction should allow the Holy Ghost to work through the Word. According to Romans 10, 17 faith comes out of preaching, or literally, out of hearing. And it is possible that through looking and drawing the true ability to hear is endangered. That there are dangers here is not to be denied, and we should point them out whenever we discover them. However it would be a fatal illogicality to draw from the true *theological* proposition that Christian teaching is concerned with a hearing community the *didactic* conclusion that only talking is permitted. Kurt Frör (ed). *Das Zeichnen im kirchlichen Unterricht* (München 1958), 20-1

4.9.3 Buddhism and popular fears

Because of ignorance the three worlds are a prison,
Because of enlightenment the ten directions are free.

In truth there is neither East nor West,
Where then are South and North?

G. Renondeau. *Le Shugendô* : *Historie, Doctrine et Rites des Anachonetes dits Yamabushi.* Cahiers de la Société Asiatique 8 (Paris 1964), 140

This spell, once used by wandering Japanese monks, both accepts the popular belief that certain quarters of the compass are under the malevolent influence of demons, and at the same time rejects it with a reference to Buddhist philosophy.

4.9.4 Mao Tse-tung as a Buddhist monk
I am a lone monk walking the world with a leaky umbrella. *The Sunday Times,* 2 May 1971 (interview with Chairman Mao by Edgar Snow)

4.10 RELIGIOUS THEORIES OF RELIGION
Religions display from their inception ad hoc attitudes towards other beliefs and practices in the context in which they arise, and such attitudes are mostly polemical. The Koran, for example, inveighs against 'idolaters', Buddhist writings reflect sharp disagreement with other Indian sects, and so on. As more comprehensive theories of 'other' religions are worked out in a developing tradition, these tend to say more about the religion which is the starting point than about the real nature of the 'other' religions. Various theories should be expected within a single tradition, reflecting variations of theological emphasis. There are two lines of thought within Islam, for example, one insisting that the revelations to the prophet supersede all others, and the other preferring to emphasise a mystical unity of all religions. The latter view is widely shared in Asia, but not universally.

4.10.1 Jesus on religion

'Alas for you, lawyers and Pharisees, hypocrites! You are like tombs covered with whitewash; they look well from outside, but inside they are full of dead men's bones and all kinds of filth. So it is with you : outside you look like honest men, but inside you are brimful of hypocrisy and crime . . .

'O Jerusalem, Jerusalem, the city that murders the prophets and stones the messengers sent to her! How often have I longed to gather your children, as a hen gathers her brood under her wings; but you would not let me. Look, look! there is your temple, forsaken by God . . .' Matthew xxiii, 27-8, 37-8

4.10.2 Justin solves a problem

Lest some should unreasonably object, in order to turn men away from what we teach, that we say that Christ was born a hundred and fifty years ago under Quirinius, and taught what we say he taught still later, under Pontius Pilate, and should accuse us [as supposing] that all men born before that time were irresponsible, I will solve this difficulty in advance. We have been taught that Christ is the First-begotten of God, and have previously testified that he is the Reason of which every race of man partakes. Those who lived in accordance with Reason are Christians, even though they were called godless, such as, among the Greeks, Socrates and Heraclitus and others like them; among the barbarians, Abraham, Ananiah, Azariah, and Mishael, and Elijah, and many others, whose deeds and names I forbear to list, knowing that this would be lengthy. So also those who lived without Reason were ungracious and enemies to Christ, and murderers of those who lived by Reason. But those who lived by Reason, and those who so live now, are Christians, fearless and unperturbed. Cyril C. Richardson (et al). *Early Christian Fathers*. Library of Christian Classics Vol I (1953), 271-2 (First Apology of Justin 46)

'Reason', ie *logos*.

4.10.3 The Koran on religion

And the Jews say : Ezra is the son of Allah, and the Christians
say : The Messiah is the son of Allah. That is their saying with
their mouths. They imitate the saying of those who disbelieved
of old. Allah (himself) fighteth against them. How perverse are
they!

They have taken as lords beside Allah their rabbis and
their monks and the Messiah son of Mary, when they were
bidden to worship only One God. There is no god save Him.
Be He glorified from all that they ascribe as partner (unto
Him)!

Fain would they put out the light of Allah with their mouths,
but Allah disdaineth (aught) save that he shall perfect His light,
however much the disbelievers are averse.

He it is who hath sent his messenger with the guidance and
the Religion of Truth, that He may cause it to prevail over all
religion, however much the idolaters may be averse. Pickthall.
The Meaning of the Glorious Koran, 148 (Sūrah ix, 30-3)

The phrase 'be he glorified from all . . .' is no more clearly translated by Arberry. George Sale, in 1734, translated, 'far be that
from him, which they associate *with him*!' (*The Koran* (1734,
1899), 138).

4.10.4 Rūmī on religion

Though the roads are various, the goal is one. Do you not see
that there are many roads to the Kaaba? For some the road is
from Rum, for some from Syria, for some from Persia, for some
from China, for some by sea from India and Yemen. So if you
consider the roads, the variety is great and the divergence infinite; but when you consider the goal, they are all of one accord
and one. The hearts of all are at one upon the Kaaba. The
hearts have one attachment, an ardour and a great love for the
Kaaba, and in that there is no room for contrariety. That attachment is neither infidelity nor faith; that is to say, that attachment is not confounded with the various roads which we have

mentioned. Once they have arrived there, that disputation and war and diversity touching the roads—this man saying to that man, 'You are false, you are an infidel,' and the other replying in kind—once they have arrived at the Kaaba, it is realised that that warfare was concerning the roads only, and that their goal was one . . .

All men say, 'We will enter the Kaaba.' Some men say, 'If God wills, we will enter.' Those who use the expression 'if God wills' are the true lovers of God. For the lover does not consider himself in charge of things and a free agent; he recognises that the Beloved is in charge. Hence he says, 'If the Beloved wills, I will enter.'

Now the literalists take the Holy Mosque to be that Kaaba to which people repair. Lovers, however, and the elect of God, take the Holy Mosque to mean union with God. Arberry. *Discourses of Rūmī,* 109 and 111

The Kaaba is the central sanctuary of Islam at Mecca, but the thirteenth century Persian mystic intends it to mean mystical union with God. By playing on the term Kaaba however he seeks to make his vision of the profound unity of different religions acceptable in orthodox Muslim terms.

4.10.5 Gurū Nānak on religion

I have consulted the four Veds, but these writings find not God's
      limits.
I have consulted the four books *of the Muhammadans,* but
      God's worth is not described in them.
I have consulted the nine regions of the earth; one improveth
      upon what the other saith.
Having turned my heart into a boat, I have searched in every
      sea;
I have dwelt by rivers and streams, and bathed at the sixty-eight
      places of pilgrimage;
I have lived among the forests and glades of the three worlds
      and eaten bitter and sweet;

I have seen the seven nether regions and heavens upon heavens. *And I*, Nānak, *say* man shall be true to his faith if he fear *God* and *do good* works.
M. A. Macauliffe. *The Sikh Religion* Vol I (Delhi 1963), 179

It is often supposed that the Sikh religion is a synthesis of Hinduism and Islam, and with regard to some of its characteristics it perhaps is. Yet for Gurū Nānak, as W. H. Mcleod points out (*Gurū Nānak and the Sikh Religion* (Oxford 1968), 161), 'True religion lay beyond these two systems, accessible to all men of spiritual perception whether Hindu or Muslim.' Cf 4.10.6.

4.10.6   Gurū Gobind Singh on religion

Vishnu, the Lord of Lakshmi, cannot find his limit; the Veds and the books of the Musalmans cannot utter his secret . . .

The Veds, the Purans, the Quran, and other Muhammedan books have grown weary of taking God's account, but they have not found it.

Without the light of true love hath any one obtained the honour of finding God? Macauliffe. *The Sikh Religion,* Vol V, 280-1

Cf 4.10.5. The present quotation shows that the attitude of Gurū Nānak persisted clearly in the Sikh religion.

———

PART FIVE

Complex Comparisons

As explained above (Introduction, p 23) the purpose of this section is to illustrate the possibility of extending the process of comparison beyond the four main aspects of religion, treated separately, to a more complex level. Under the headings below are given examples of the ways in which the four main aspects may be comparably related. In the past comparative studies have sometimes been rather vague about what was being compared with what, and which aspects of the total datum were being ignored. Admittedly everything cannot be done at once and comparison may fairly be expected to proceed step by step. Nevertheless there may be some value in systematically charting what in principle may be possible. The examples below, although severely selective, give some indication of the kind of steps which may be made; and for the sake of argument, cases have been adduced for each of the eleven possible correlations between the four main aspects of religion.

5.1 CONCEPTS AND ACTION

Religious action and religious concepts are very closely related indeed. To consider religious action phenomenologically means taking seriously the intentions and hence the concepts of those who perform it. Religious thought on the other hand is itself only to be understood in the total context of religious behaviour. Nevertheless, while this unity of thought and action is often insisted on in the religions themselves (5.1.1-3), the two are also frequently found in tension as when established religious action is criticised, more or less sharply, on religious grounds. (5.1.4-7).

5.1.1   The unity of meditation and wisdom

Good friends, my teaching of the Dharma takes meditation (*ting*) and wisdom (*hui*) as its basis. Never under any circumstances say mistakenly that meditation and wisdom are different; they are a unity, not two things. Meditation itself is the substance of wisdom; wisdom itself is the function of meditation. At the very moment when there is wisdom, then meditation exists in wisdom; at the very moment when there is meditation, then wisdom exists in meditation. Yampolsky. *The Platform Sutra of the Sixth Patriarch,* 135

5.1.2   The unity of theory and practice

Any separation of theory from practice leads to errors, to throwbacks in the class struggle and to obstacles and disturbances in the building-up of socialism. Theory always has to reflect the developing practice in a lively way, and by the analysis of practice it has to work out what conditions are required for the further development of society. Marxism rejects any philosophising and theorising estranged from practice and reality.

With the founding of dialectical materialism philosophy has stopped being a mere interpretation of the world, setting up abstract social ideals. Through its application by the working class it became a means for the revolutionary restructuring of the world. The basic difference between dialectical-materialist philosophy and all earlier philosophies was summed up by Marx in the famous eleventh thesis on Feuerbach as follows: 'Philosophers have only variously interpreted the world; what matters

is to change it.' R. O. Gropp. *Der dialektische Materialismus*
(Leipzig 1961), 22

5.1.3 The unity of doctrine and life

A theology which . . . does not make an artificial separation
between doctrine and life, knowing and doing, theory and
practice; which holds no brief for, on the one hand, impractical
intellectualist dogmatising, divorced from life, nor, on the other,
uninspiring, casuistical, pragmatic moralising, but which works
from the conviction that God's gracious Word is always, at the
same time, a word of command making its claim and its demand upon man—dogmatics and ethics in one . . . Hans Küng.
The Theologian and the Church (1965), 12-13

5.1.4 A new covenant

Behold the days are coming, says the LORD, when I will make
a new covenant with the house of Israel and the house of Judah,
not like the covenant which I made when I took them by the
hand to lead them out of the land of Egypt, my covenant which
I broke, though I was their husband, says the LORD. But this is
the covenant which I will make with the house of Israel after
those days, says the LORD : I will put my law within them, and
I will write it upon their hearts; and I will be their God, and
they shall be my people. And no longer shall each man teach his
neighbour and each his brother, saying, 'Know the LORD,' for
they shall all know me, from the least of them to the greatest,
says the LORD; for I will forgive their iniquity, and I will remember their sin no more. Jeremiah xxxi, 31-4

5.1.5 Use of the Sabbath

One Sabbath he [Jesus] was going through the cornfields; and
his disciples, as they went, began to pluck ears of corn. The
Pharisees said to him, 'Look, why are they doing what is forbidden on the Sabbath?' He answered, 'Have you never read
what David did when he and his men were hungry and had
nothing to eat? He went into the House of God, in the time of

Abiathar the High Priest, and ate the consecrated loaves, though no one but a priest is allowed to eat them, and even gave them to his men.'

He also said to them, 'The Sabbath was made for the sake of man and not man for the Sabbath: therefore the Son of Man is sovereign even over the Sabbath.' Mark ii, 23-8

5.1.6   Islamic practice reviewed

Make kindness thy mosque, sincerity thy prayer-carpet, what is just and lawful thy Quran.

Modesty thy circumcision, civility thy fasting, so shalt thou be a Musulman . . . Macauliffe. *The Sikh Religion,* Vol I, 39

Attributed to Gurū Nānak, founder of the Sikh religion.

5.1.7   Buddhist teaching

A monk said to Joshu, 'I have just entered this monastery. I beg you to teach me.' Joshu asked, 'Have you eaten your rice-gruel?' 'I have,' replied the monk. 'Then,' said Joshu, 'go and wash your bowl(s).' The monk was enlightened. Blyth. *Zen and Zen Classics,* 81 (Mumonkan, Case VII)

5.2   ACTION AND STATES OF MIND

Faithful repetition is one of the keynotes of religious action, and this may be significant for the achievement of certain states of mind, irrespective of variations in conceptual content. Specified formulae, even if only partly understood, give re-assurance and conviction. Simple but highly routinised recita-tion can be a prelude to the achievement of visions and of mystical states. (Cf 1.6 and 4.4)

5.2.1   Creed of Saint Athanasius

Whosoever will be saved: before all things it is necessary that he hold the Catholick Faith.

Which Faith except everyone do keep whole and undefiled: without doubt he shall perish everlastingly.

And the Catholick Faith is this: that we worship one God in Trinity, and Trinity in Unity;

Neither confounding the Persons: nor dividing the Substance.

For there is one Person of the Father, another of the Son: and another of the Holy Ghost.

But the Godhead of the Father, of the Son and of the Holy Ghost, is all one: the Glory equal, the Majesty coeternal.

Such as the Father is, such is the Son: and such is the Holy Ghost.

The Father uncreate, the Son uncreate: and the Holy Ghost uncreate.

The Father incomprehensible, the Son incomprehensible: and the Holy Ghost incomprehensible.

The Father eternal, the Son eternal: and the Holy Ghost eternal.

And yet they are not three eternals: but one eternal.

As also there are not three incomprehensibles, nor three un-created: but one uncreated, and one incomprehensible.

So likewise the Father is Almighty, the Son Almighty: and the Holy Ghost Almighty . . . *Book of Common Prayer,* from 'At Morning Prayer'

This creed is sung or said instead of the Apostles' Creed on certain occasions.

5.2.2 Chanting the holy names

At dawn some of the devotees were up. They saw the master, naked as a child, pacing up and down the room, repeating the names of the various gods and goddesses. His voice was sweet as nectar. Now he would look at the Ganges, now stop in front of the pictures hanging on the wall and bow down before them, chanting all the while the holy names in his sweet voice. He chanted: 'Veda, Purāna, Tantra; Gītā, Gāyatri; Bhāgavata, Bhakta, Bhagavān.' Referring to the *Gītā,* he repeated many times, 'Tāgi, tāgi, tāgi.' Now and then he would say : 'O Mother, Thou are verily Brahman, and Thou art verily Śakti. Thou art Purusha and Thou art Prakriti. Thou art Virāt. Thou art the Absolute, and Thou dost manifest Thyself as the Relative. Thou art verily the twenty-four cosmic principles.' . . . With a sweet smile on his lips, Sri Ramakrishna was standing on the north-east verandah . . . Gupta. *The Gospel of Sri Ramakrishna,* 123

'Tāgi' is an anagram of 'Gītā' and means 'one who has renounced'.

5.2.3   Exhortation to repetition

Go on with your preaching. Cobbler, stick to your last; preacher, stick to your preaching. In the great day, when the muster roll shall be read, of all those who are converted through fine music, and church decoration, and religious exhibitions and entertainments, they will amount to the tenth part of nothing; but it will always please God by the foolishness of preaching to save them that believe. Keep to your preaching; and if you do anything beside, do not let it throw your preaching into the background. In the first place preach and in the second place preach and in the third place preach.

Believe in preaching the love of Christ, believe in preaching the atoning sacrifice, believe in preaching the new birth, believe in preaching the whole counsel of God. The old hammer of the Gospel will still break the rock in pieces; the ancient fire of Pentecost will still burn among the multitude. Try nothing new, but go on with preaching, and if we all preach with the Holy Ghost sent down from heaven, the results of preaching will astound us . . . Robert H. Thouless. *An Introduction to the Psychology of Religion* (Cambridge 1923), 150 (quoting words of the preacher Spurgeon given in a book by R. A. Torrey entitled *How to Promote and Conduct a Successful Revival*)

5.2.4   Sutra-reading

The sutra-reading in the Buddhist monasteries can thus be

reckoned as a sort of prayer. The reading, even when its full
meaning is not grasped, detaches one's mind from worldly con-
cerns and self-centred interests. Though negative, the merit here-
with gained tends to direct the mind towards the attainment of
Sarvajñatā . . .

As the Mahā-prajñā-pāramitā sutras are of such a bulk, they
cannot be finished within a prescribed period. The six hundred
volumes are divided among the monks and each monk reads two
or three pages in the beginning and at the end of each volume
while the middle part is read by turning over the entire volume
for a few times; hence the phrase 'read by revolving'. Suzuki.
The Training of the Zen Buddhist Monk, 77-8

5.3 ACTION AND GROUPS

Rites concerned with puberty and adolescence, ie rites of
'initiation' into adulthood, are usually to be found in simple
group or civil religion. They should be distinguished from rites
of initiation into the more specialised minor group religions
(cf 5.7), even though there tends to be some interplay between
these different types (cf 6.5). Many rites of this kind described
by anthropologists last for many days or months or even
years.

5.3.1 Puberty and warriorhood

After his circumcision a boy is secluded in his house for two
days. Then he leaves the house early in the morning to join his
confreres and go into the forest for the day. Each boy has a bow
and a supply of arrows, prepared before the ceremony, with
which he shoots birds and small animals. The birds are stuffed
and tied to the edge of a wooden hoop which is worn as a ceremonial headdress at dances . . . In each ward of the village one
house is set aside for the circumcised boys of the ward to sleep
in. During this period of ceremonial hunting these boys eat together of food brought to them by their parents. In the evenings
they learn special songs which they sing at their own initiations,

and later at other ceremonies in which their age-set participates.

Circumcision confers a new ritual status on a Sonjo boy—for one thing, he is no longer strictly forbidden sexual intercourse on the grounds of being impure—and qualifies him for initiation into the warrior class . . . After the ceremonial hunting period is finished he goes back to his old duties of herding goats for one or two years until his initiation . . . The fathers of all the candidates slaughter goats for feasting and prepare large quantities of beer . . . The candidates themselves are given instruction in the duties of warriors; then they are shaved and prepared to participate in two ceremonial dances on consecutive days. On the first day they discard their headdresses, the birds being given to young children to play with, and their old garments . . . On the second day they are formally acknowledged to be warriors. Robert F. Gray. *The Sonjo of Tanganyika, An Anthropological Study of an Irrigation-based Society* (1963), 86-7

5.3.2 Bar Mitzvah prayer

Prayer recited by the Bar Mitzvah, when called to the Law, before the Blessing; or after his being addressed by the Minister.

Heavenly Father, at this sacred and solemn hour of my life I stand before thee in the midst of this holy congregation, to declare my duty ever to turn to thee in daily prayer, and to observe the commandments of thy Law by which a man may live worthily. I pray humbly and hopefully before thee to grant me thy gracious help, so that I have the will and the understanding to walk firmly in thy ways all the days of my life. Implant in me a spirit of sincere devotion to thy service, that I may hold fast to what is holy and just and good, and resist all evil and sinful temptations.

As I grow into full manhood, under thy loving care, may bodily strength, mental power and moral courage be developed in me, that I may fulfil my duties to thee with reverence, knowledge and love, as well as my duties to my neighbour, with zeal, sympathy and courtesy.

Today I enter the community, as one worthy to be numbered to form a congregation for public worship, and to assume the full responsibilities of a Jew. Help me, O merciful Father, who hast chosen thy people Israel for thy service, ever to be numbered and known as a faithful son of thy people, zealous for its fair name and proud to share in the burden of the heritage of the congregation of Jacob. Aid my resolve never to separate myself from the community but always to regard myself as a member of the people of Israel, whose welfare and glory it will be my task to maintain and enhance.

May the noble example of our ancestors inspire me always to be ready to sanctify thy Name, and to witness thy protection and care which extend to all thy works. Amen. Brodie. *The Authorised Daily Prayer Book of the United Hebrew Congregations of the British Commonwealth of Nations*, 407-8

The central part of the Jewish coming of age ceremony is when the boy concerned reads a passage from the Torah (Law) before the assembled community in the synagogue.

_____

5.4 GROUPS AND STATES OF MIND

Although the cases given below are fairly dramatic, it may be noted that *some* relationship between religious states of mind and social groupings is *always* to be sought. It is for this reason that matters such as 'conversion' or 'mysticism' cannot really be treated just as 'experience' or even simply as a correlation of states of mind and doctrine. Specific types of religious group are clearly conducive to, and in turn dependent on, the arousal of states associated with them. In the examples given the concepts entertained are quite various, and there are also varying degrees of self-conscious routinisation.

_____

5.4.1 Sri Ramakrishna and followers

About eight o'clock in the morning Sri Ramakrishna went as planned to Balaram Bose's house in Calcutta. It was the day of

L

the Dolayātrā. Ram, Manomohan, Rakhal, Nityagopal, and other devotees were with him. M., too, came, as bidden by the Master.

The devotees and the Master sang and danced in a state of divine fervour. Several of them were in an ecstatic mood. Nityagopal's chest glowed with the upsurge of emotion, and Rakhal lay on the floor in ecstasy, completely unconscious of the world. The Master put his hand on Rakhal's chest and said : 'Peace. Be quiet.' This was Rakhal's first experience of ecstasy. Gupta. *The Gospel of Sri Ramakrishna,* 93

Dolayātrā is the Hindu spring festival associated with Sri Krishna. 'M' is the pseudonym of Mahendranath Gupta, who wrote the account of Sri Ramakrishna's conversations. The above account is dated 1882.

5.4.2 Bektashi wine and dance
Come O cup-bearer of the unity, offer the cup of wine, *payale.*
'Their Lord shall cause them to drink pure water.'
From its brim may life come to the people of ecstasy.
'Their Lord shall cause them to drink pure water.' . . .

From its wine [ie, the drinking of the rite] the people of hearts
    being intoxicated and bewildered
Overflow like the seven seas.
From eternity we have drunk that cup
Overflowing like the seven seas.

May it take away the barrier of the people of hearts
May it reveal the moonlight of hearts
Bring to the *meydan* that wine of *Kevser*
May it reveal the moonlight of hearts. . . .

As they eat and drink musicians play upon stringed instruments . . . Then those who wish rise for the dance, *sema,* which is done in couples, a man and a woman together . . . the first 'figure' consists of rhythmically bending their bodies to the right and left, at first slowly then with increased speed. In the second 'figure' they put their left hands on their breasts, bow slightly, then as their bodies bend, swing also their arms from right to left and back. In the third 'figure' they move around, *devreder-ler*. After encircling the room a few times they come to the fourth 'figure' in which each turns as they together move about the room, the music quickening and becoming louder. John Kingsley Birge. *The Bektashi Order of Dervishes* (1965), 200-1 and 199

The quotation in the first stanza is Quran 76:21 (compare the whole context). The 'wine of Kevser' is a marvellous drink from a pool in Paradise, to be drunk on the day of Resurrection, and here brought already to the place of ceremonial. The 'people of hearts' are those guided by inner experience, and the 'barrier' is the 'veil' which would prevent them from receiving manifestations of divine reality. The poem is recited before the sharing of wine and the dance. The latter is of course comparable to that of the famous Mevlevi dervishes who whirl in a special manner to the accompaniment of music.

5.4.3 The Japanese 'Dancing Religion'

The Prayer of Odoru Shukyo is said in a remarkable way—in fact it is 'spoken' with the whole body. The believers work themselves into complete religious ecstasy, tears run down their cheeks, and their limbs vibrate. They shake their hands and lift them above their heads again and again with vehement movements. In the *Prophet of Tabuse* it is explained as follows :

'In the beginning Ogamisama prayed *Namu myoho renge kyo* to expel evil spirits, but later on, all the comrades joined her in prayer. During the course of one such earnest prayer a most wonderful phenomenon occurred among the comrades. Their clasped hands quivered up and down involuntarily as they prayed. At first they were surprised at these unaccountable movements, but Ogamisama explained that "It is a psychic activity. When your hands are shaking high at your breast it means that your living spirit is activated. When the unconverted or stray spirits of the dead influence you, your hands will shift downward and will make downward movements. But as soon as these spirits are converted or leave you for the moment, your hands will rise above your head." ' Harry Thomsen. *The New Religions of Japan* (Rutland, Vermont 1963), 208

'Ogamisama' is the title given to the foundress of this religion popularly known as 'Odoru Shukyo' or 'Dancing Religion'. *The Prophet of Tabuse* was published by the headquarters of the religion itself, at Tabuse in 1954. *'Namu myoho renge kyo'* is the invocation of the title of the Lotus Sutra, though this religion is not itself so closely associated with the sutra as others are. The dance is sometimes described as expressing *muga* or 'non-self'.

5.4.4 A revival in Kentucky

The whole body of persons who actually fell helpless to the earth during the progress of the meeting was computed . . . to be three thousand persons, about one in every six . . . 'At no time was the floor less than half covered. Some lay quiet, unable to move or speak. Some talked, but could not move. Some beat the floor with their heels. Some, shrieking in agony, bounded about like a live fish out of water. Many lay down and rolled over and over for hours at a time. Others rushed wildly over the stumps and benches, and then plunged, shouting, 'Lost! Lost!' into the forest.' . . . Next to the 'falling' exercise the most notable and characteristic Kentucky phenomenon was the 'jerks.' The unhappy victim shook in every joint. Sometimes the head was thrown from side to side with great rapidity. Again the feet were affected, and the subject would hop like a frog. Often the body would be thrown violently to the ground, where it would continue to bound from one place to another. Peter Cartwright declares that he has seen more than five hundred persons jerking at once in the congregation . . . Another phenomenon not so common was the 'barking' exercise. The votaries of this dignified rite gathered in groups on all fours, like dogs, growling and snapping their teeth at the foot of a tree as the minister preached —a practice which they designated as 'treeing the devil' ! . . . Many of these camp-meeting folk lay insensible, sometimes for hours, but when they recovered from the swoon it was to relate, in what were called 'strains of heaven,' experiences of inter-views with departed friends and visions of glory. Thouless. *An Introduction to the Psychology of Religion,* 155 (quoting Daven-port, *Primitive Traits in Religious Revivals* (New York 1906), 77-80)

This revival took place in 1801.

5.4.5 Revival experience from the inside

I had been carefully trained, and had received more than an ordinary amount of religious and biblical instruction. The winter that I was 11, a series of revival meetings was being held, to which I was taken. I attended some half-dozen without receiv-ing any impression. At the very last meeting the usual appeal was made for those to rise who wished to be on the Lord's side. There was considerable excitement. In the midst of it I rose and remained standing. I think I had no conscious motive in taking this step. I was simply carried away by the excitement, and did not know what I did. If any influence came in, it was love for my mother, who sat beside me, bowed in prayer. I felt that she wished me to rise, and yet the knowledge was something I felt after rather than before I rose. I was much excited, and became hysterical under the emotions aroused and under the prevailing excitement . . . I was taken apart with others and talked with, and as a result joined the P— church the next Sunday . . . The experiences had been unnatural, and therefore could not last. I lived for a short time, perhaps six months, under an unnatural excitement, and then relapsed into a state of utter indifference. Starbuck. *The Psychology of Religion,* 166

5.5   STATES OF MIND AND CONCEPTS

Certitude of conviction is a common and important facet of religious feeling which is naturally related to the formulation and tradition of religious concepts. This is sometimes explicitly recognised by religious persons themselves, as in the cases below, but its role in what are sometimes thought to be 'non-dogmatic' religions such as Zen Buddhism (cf 1.10.2 and 3.1.3), and in mysticism generally (cf 3.3 and 3.4) is not always noticed.

5.5.1   Shinran's faith

I will have no regrets even though I should have been deceived by Hōnen Shōnin, and thus by uttering the Nembutsu, I should fall into hell. The reason is that, if I could become Buddha by performing some other practice and fell into hell by uttering the Nembutsu, then, I might feel regret at having been deceived. But since I am incapable of any practice whatsoever, hell would definitely be my dwelling anyway.

If the Original Vow of Amida is true, then Śakyamuni's sermons cannot be untrue. If the Buddha's words are true, then Zendō's comments cannot be untrue. If Zendō's comments are true, how can Hōnen's sayings be false? If Hōnen's sayings are true, what I, Shinran, say cannot possibly be false. After all is said, such is the faith of this simpleton [myself]. Beyond this, it is entirely left up to each one of you whether you accept and believe in the Nembutsu or reject it. Thus it was said. *The Tanni Shō, Notes Lamenting Differences,* Ryukoku Translation Series II (Kyoto 1963), 20-1

The Nembutsu is the invocation of the name of Amida (Amitābha) Buddha in response to the latter's vow to save all beings who rely on him in sincere faith.

5.5.2   Positive preaching

Revival preaching to be effective must be positive. The doubter

never has revivals . . . A revival is a revolution in many important respects, and revolutions are never brought about by timid,
fearful or deprecatory addresses. They are awakened by men
who are cocksure of their ground, and who speak with authority
. . . Revival preaching must be directed towards the heart and
not the head . . . Get hold of the heart and the head yields easily.
Thouless. *An Introduction to the Psychology of Religion,* 149
(quoting R. A. Torrey, *How to Promote and Conduct a Successful Revival,* 32)

5.6 GROUPS AND CONCEPTS

One of the more obvious facts about the relation between
religious groups and concepts is that the main divisions of the
social shape of religion given above (2.1-5) seem to correspond
to certain conceptual emphases. Simple group religion is characterised above all by its reference to a powerful central symbol, while civil religion also has such a symbol or symbols but
articulates more deliberately a complex hierarchy of authoritative figures and perhaps a certain elementary morality. Minor
group religions are explicitly or implicitly critical of the ordinary daily world of human life, although they may be world-
affirming in a deeper sense; in contrast to civil religion they
offer some alternative electionist, salvationist, perfectionist or
utopian focus of interest. Folk religion is mainly concerned
with miscellaneous benefits such as protection from misfortune,
healing and personal prosperity. Of course this analysis is
highly stylised and in general terms it is already sufficiently
illustrated by the data given in part two above.

Change in the social shape of religion and change in its conceptual content go hand in hand. If the religion of a minor
group becomes so powerful that within a clearly defined area
it becomes a civil religion in its own right, then some conceptual ambivalence is to be expected. This has frequently
happened in the case of Christianity. Another significant kind
of interplay between conceptual and social change is the

assimilation of simple groups under a common mythology, and this is illustrated below in 5.6.1 and 5.6.2.

5.6.1   Joshua's covenant at Shechem

'Now therefore fear the Lord, and serve him in sincerity and in faithfulness; put away the gods which your fathers served beyond the River, and in Egypt, and serve the Lord. And if you be unwilling to serve the Lord, choose this day whom you will serve, whether the gods your fathers served in this region beyond the River, or the gods of the Amorites in whose land you dwell; but as for me and my house, we will serve the Lord.'

Then the people answered, 'Far be it from us that we should forsake the Lord, to serve other gods; for it is the Lord our God who brought us and our fathers up from the land of Egypt, out of the house of bondage, and who did those great signs in our sight, and preserved us in all the way that we went, and among all the peoples through whom we passed; and the Lord drove out before us all the peoples, the Amorites who lived in the land; therefore we also will serve the Lord, for he is our God.'

But Joshua said to the people, 'You cannot serve the Lord; for he is a holy God; he is a jealous God; he will not forgive your transgressions or your sins. If you forsake the Lord and serve foreign gods, then he will turn and do you harm, and consume you, after having done you good.' And the people said to Joshua, 'Nay; but we will serve the Lord.' Then Joshua said to the people, 'You are witnesses against yourselves that you have chosen the Lord, to serve him.' And they said, 'We are witnesses.' He said, 'Then put away the foreign gods which are among you, and incline your heart to the Lord, the God of Israel.' And the people said to Joshua, 'The Lord our God we will serve, and his voice we will obey.' So Joshua made a covenant with the people that day, and made statutes and ordinances for them at Shechem. Joshua xxiv, 14-25

It is thought that at the time of the conquest of Palestine in the late thirteenth century BC, not only the immigrants who actually carried with them the tradition of the Exodus, but also various miscellaneous groups of people, some of whom were resident in Palestine from before, came to be associated together in the Israelite tribal confederation. The focal point of this confederation was the covenant with Yahweh. Cf John Bright. *A History of Israel* (1960), 145.

5.6.2 Deities produced by Izanagi

Moreover, the Deities which were produced by his plunging down and washing in the bottom of the sea were called Soko-tsu-wata-tsu-mi no Mikoto and Soko-tsutsu-wo no Mikoto. Moreover, when he plunged and washed in the mid-tide, there were Gods produced who were called Naka tsu wata-dzu-mi no Mikoto, and next Naka-tsutsu-wo no Mikoto. Moreover, when he washed floating on the surface of the water, Gods were produced who were called Uha-tsu-wata-dzu-mi no Mikoto and next Uha-tsutsu-wo no Mikoto. There were in all nine Gods. The Gods Soko-tsutsu-wo no Mikoto, Naka-tsutsu-wo no Mikoto, and Suha-tsutsu-wo no Mikoto are the three great Gods of Suminoye. The Gods Soko-tsu-wata-dzu-mi no Mikoto, Naka-tsu-wata-dzu-mi no Mikoto, and Uha-tsu-wata-dzu-mi no Mikoto are the Gods worshipped by the Muraji of Adzumi. Aston. *Nihongi*, 27

This passage continues that quoted above (1.3.2). The names of the divinities are stylised, and there is some confusion over both names and numbers; however the implication that Izanagi's purification was the origin of various ancestral gods here linked together seems clear. On a larger scale, whole independent myth cycles seem to have been woven together under the dominant Amaterasu story, in the *Kojiki* and *Nihongi* (cf J. H. Kamstra. *Encounter or Syncretism,* Leiden 1967), which were official productions of the ascendant Yamato clan.

5.7   ACTION, CONCEPTS AND GROUPS

If simple group religion or civil religion have fundamentally
a world-affirming attitude and minor group religions display
a more or less critical attitude towards the world in general
and offer their own alternatives (cf 5.6) it is not surprising if
this distinction is reflected also in the religious action typical
of each. It is noticeable that simple group or civil religion
usually provides ritual for the main crises of life such as
birth, adolescence and marriage, and death, and for occupational and other occasional needs (cf 1.7 and 5.3). Minor
group religions, however, typically have two main rites, an
initiatory rite, and a recapitulating or intensifying rite. The
initiatory rites of this class should be carefully distinguished
from the adolescence rites of civil religion, even though there
is much interplay between the two (cf 5.3 and 6.4). Distinc-
tions made here are often blurred by the fact that a single
religious tradition may change its social position in the
course of time (cf 6.4). The extracts below represent the
initiatory rites of minor group religions which all involve the
concept of entering a special community, but which are
otherwise conducive to highly divergent states of mind. 5.7.5
is a recapitulatory rite; the equivalent Christian rite being
the eucharist (cf 1.2.3 and 1.4.5); and the equivalent
Buddhist rite being the *uposatha* including confession of
offences and recitation of the *patimokkh*a rules (cf the con-
venient account in Thomas' *The History of Buddhist
Thought* (1951), 15-22).

5.7.1   Consecration of a priest

The high priest who is to be consecrated is brought down under
ground in a pit dug deep, marvellously adorned with a fillet,
binding his festive temples with chaplets, his hair combed back
under a golden crown, and wearing a silken toga caught up
with Gabine girding.

Over this they make a wooden floor with wide spaces, woven

of planks with an open mesh; they then divide or bore the area
and repeatedly pierce the wood with a pointed tool that it may
appear full of small holes.

Hither a huge bull, fierce and shaggy in appearance, is led,
bound with flowery garlands about its flanks, and with its
horns sheathed; yea, the forehead of the victim sparkles with
gold, and the flash of metal plates colours its hair.

Here, as is ordained, the beast is to be slain, and they pierce
its breast with a sacred spear; the gaping wound emits a wave
of hot blood, and the smoking river flows into the woven
structure beneath it and surges wide.

Then by the many paths of the thousand openings in the
lattice the falling shower rains down a foul dew, which the
priest buried within catches, putting his shameful head under
all the drops, defiled both in his clothing and in all his body.

Yea, he throws back his face, he puts his cheeks in the way
of the blood, he puts under it his ears and lips, he interposes
his nostrils, he washes his very eyes with the fluid, nor does he
even spare his throat but moistens his tongue, until he actually
drinks the dark gore.

Afterwards, the flamens draw the corpse, stiffening now that
the blood has gone forth, off the lattice, and the pontiff,
horrible in appearance, comes forth, and shows his wet head,
his beard heavy with blood, his dripping fillets and sodden
garments.

This man, defiled with such contagions and foul with the
gore of the recent sacrifice, all hail and worship at a distance,
because profane blood and a dead ox have washed him while
concealed in a filthy cave. C. K. Barrett. *The New Testament
Background: Selected Documents* (1958), 96-7 (quoting
Prudentius' *Peristephanon* x, 1011-50)

This is an unsympathetic but circumstantial description of a
rite intended in this case to consecrate a priest in the cult of the
'Great Mother' (Cybele), but also used as an initiation in
Mithraism.

5.7.2 Christian baptism

Almighty, everliving God, whose most dearly beloved Son Jesus Christ, for the forgiveness of our sins, did shed out of his most precious side both water and blood, and gave commandment to his disciples, that they should go teach all nations, and baptise them In the Name of the Father, the Son, and the Holy Ghost; Regard, we beseech thee, the supplications of this congregation; sanctify this Water to the mystical washing away of sin; and grant that the *persons* now to be baptised therein may receive the fulness of thy grace, and ever remain in the number of thy faithful and elect children, through Jesus Christ our Lord. *Amen.*

Then shall the Priest take each person to be baptised by the right hand, and placing him conveniently by the Font, according to his discretion, shall ask the Godfathers and Godmothers the Name; and then shall dip him in the water, or pour water upon him, saying,

N. I baptise thee in the Name of the Father, and of the Son, and of the Holy Ghost. Amen. *Book of Common Prayer,* from 'The Ministration of Baptism to such as are of Riper years and able to answer for themselves'.

This rite is clearly intended to be a sacrament of initiation into the special body of the elect, even though it is part of the order of the established Church of England in which infant baptism has been a general social requirement (cf 6.5.4).

5.7.3 Initiation in the Qumran community (i)

No candidate, however, is to be admitted to the formal state of purity enjoyed by the general membership of the community until, at the completion of a full year, his spiritual attitude and his performance have been duly reviewed. Meanwhile he is to have no stake in the common funds.

After he has spent a full year in the midst of the community, the members are jointly to review his case, as to his understanding and performance in matters of doctrine. If it then be voted by the opinion of the priests and a majority of their co-covenanters to admit him to the sodality, they are to have him bring with him all his property and the tools of his profession . . .

Not until the completion of a second year among the members of the community is the candidate to be admitted to the common board . . . Gaster. *The Dead Sea Scriptures,* 51 (*The Manual of Discipline* vi)

Cf 5.7.4.

5.7.4 Initiation in the Qumran community (ii)

Moreover, all who would join the ranks of the community must enter into a covenant in the presence of God to do according to all that he has commanded and not to turn away from Him through any fear or terror or through any trial to which they may be subjected through the domination of Belial.

When they enter into that covenant, the priests and the levites are to pronounce a blessing upon the God of salvation and upon all that He does to make known His truth; and all that enter the covenant are to say after them, Amen, amen.

Then the priests are to rehearse the bounteous acts of God as revealed in His deeds of power, and they are to recite all His tender mercies towards Israel; while the levites are to rehearse the iniquities of the children of Israel and all the guilty transgressions and sins that they have committed through the domination of Belial. And all who enter the covenant are to make confession after them, saying, We have acted perversely . . .

Then the priests are to invoke a blessing on all that have cast their lot with God, that walk blamelessly in all their ways; and they are to say: MAY HE BLESS THEE with all good and KEEP THEE from all evil, and ILLUMINE thy heart with insight into the things of life, and GRACE THEE with knowledge of things eternal, and LIFT UP HIS gracious COUN-

TENANCE TOWARDS THEE to grant thee peace everlasting.

The levites, on the other hand, are to invoke a curse on all that have cast their lot with Belial, and to say in response: Cursed art thou for all thy wicked guilty works. May God make thee a thing of abhorrence at the hands of all who would wreak vengeance, and visit thine offspring with destruction at the hands of all who would mete out retribution. Cursed art thou, beyond hope of mercy . . .

And all that enter the covenant shall say alike after them that bless and after them that curse, Amen, amen. Gaster. *The Dead Sea Scriptures* 40-1 (*The Manual of Discipline,* i-ii)

The religious forms of this community are drawn mainly from the Judaism contemporary with it, but they were an elitist, purist and physically separatist group. *Belial* is a personification of worthlessness and wickedness. Cf 5.7.3 and 5.7.5.

5.7.5   The annual review at Qumran
The following procedure is to be followed year by year so long as Belial continues to hold sway.

The priests are first to be reviewed in due order, one after another, in respect of the state of their spirits. After them, the levites shall similarly be reviewed, and in the third place all the laity one after another, in their thousands, hundreds, fifties and tens. The object is that every man in Israel may be made aware of his status in the community of God in the sense of the ideal, eternal society, and that none may be abased below his status nor exalted above his allotted place. All of them will thus be members of a community founded at once upon true values and upon a becoming sense of humility, upon charity and mutual fairness—members of a society truly hallowed, partners in an everlasting communion. Gaster. *The Dead Sea Scriptures,* 41-2 (*The Manual of Discipline* ii)

Cf 5.7.3 and 5.7.4.

5.7.6 Buddhist ordination (i)

Then the venerable Aññāta Koṇḍañña, having seen *dhamma,* attained *dhamma,* known *dhamma,* plunged into *dhamma,* having crossed over doubt, having put away uncertainty, having attained without another's help to full confidence in the teacher's instruction, spoke thus to the Lord : 'May I, Lord, receive the going forth in the Lord's presence, may I receive ordination?'

'Come monk,' the Lord said, 'well taught is *dhamma;* fare the Brahma-faring for making an utter end of ill.' So this came to be the venerable one's ordination. I. B. Horner (trans). *Book of Discipline* IV (1951), 18-19 (*Mahāvagga* 6.32)

5.7.7 Buddhist ordination (ii)

'I allow, monks, that you yourselves may now let go forth, may ordain in any quarter in any district. And thus, monks, should one let go forth, should one ordain : First, having made him have his hair and beard cut off, having made him put on yellow robes, having made him arrange an upper robe over one shoulder, having made him honour the monks' feet, having made him sit down on his haunches, having made him salute with joined palms, he should be told : "Speak thus, I go to the awakened one for refuge, I go to *dhamma* for refuge, I go to the Order for refuge. And a second time I go . . . And a third time I go to . . . the Order for refuge ". I allow, monks, the going forth and the ordination by these three goings for refuge.' Horner. *Book of Discipline* IV, 30 (*Mahāvagga* 12.3-4)

Miss Horner notes that this transfer of competence from the Buddha to the monks seems to have been the second stage in the development of Buddhist ordination.

5.8 CONCEPTS, GROUPS AND STATES

As an example of the interplay between these three, we may note the sense of persecution sometimes felt by members of a minor group religion, which is basically similar whatever the varying style of their religious activities may be. The ideas which arise are similar in the sense that they reassure the persecuted and promise them an appropriate reward for endurance.

5.8.1 The persecuted (i)

Be at ease, O Lord. After thy complete extinction, in the horrible last period of the world, we will proclaim this sublime Sûtra.

We will suffer, patiently endure, O Lord, the injuries, threats, blows and threats with sticks at the hands of foolish men.

At that last dreadful epoch men will be malign, crooked, wicked, dull, conceited, fancying to have come to the limit when they have not . . .

Cruel-minded and wicked men, only occupied with household cares, will enter our retreat in the forest and become our calumniators.

The Tîrthikas, themselves bent on profit and honour, will say of us that we are so, and—Shame on such monks!—they will preach their own fictions.

Prompted by greed of profit and honour they will compose Sûtras of their own invention and then, in the midst of the assembly, accuse us of plagiarism . . .

And those fools who will not listen to us, shall (sooner or later) become enlightened, and therefore will we forbear to the last.

In that dreadful, most terrible period of frightful general revolution will many fiendish monks stand up as our revilers.

Out of respect for the Chief of the world we will bear it, however difficult it may be; girded with the girdle of forbearance will I proclaim this Sûtra. Kern. *Saddharma-Puṇḍarīka or The Lotus of the True Law,* 259-60

Tîrthikas are followers of rival systems, such as the Jainas.

5.8.2 The persecuted (ii)

My dear friends, do not be bewildered by the fiery ordeal that is upon you, as though it were something extraordinary. It gives you a share in Christ's sufferings, and that is cause for joy; and when his glory is revealed, your joy will be triumphant. If Christ's name is flung in your teeth as an insult, count yourselves happy, because then that glorious Spirit which is the Spirit of God is resting upon you. If you suffer, it must not be for murder, theft or sorcery, nor for infringing the rights of others. But if anyone suffers as a Christian, he should feel it no disgrace, but confess that name to the honour of God . . . And if it is hard enough for the righteous to be saved, what will become of the impious and sinful? So even those who suffer, if it be according to God's will, should commit their souls to him—by doing good; their Maker will not fail them. 1 Peter iv, 12-16, 18-19

5.8.3 The persecuted (iii)

Behold the sinners were laughing at the believers,
when they passed them by winking at one another,
and when they returned to their people they returned blithely,
and when they saw them they said, 'Lo, these men are astray!'
Yet they were not sent as watchers over them.
So today the believers are laughing at the unbelievers,
upon couches gazing.
Have the unbelievers been rewarded what they were doing? . . .

Those who persecute the believers, men and women,
and then have not repented, there awaits them the
chastisement of Gehenna, and there awaits them
the chastisement of the burning.
Those who believe, and do righteous deeds, for them
await gardens underneath which rivers flow; that is
the great triumph.

Arberry. *The Koran Interpreted* II, 330 and 332 (sura LXXXIII, 30-5, and LXXXV, 10-13)

———

M

5.9   GROUPS, STATES AND ACTION

The revival scenes and dancing religions referred to in 5.4 above already gave some idea of what may be expected under the present heading, although there the action was of a varied sort and in particular showed varying degrees of routinisation. There have been many cenobitic groups pursuing roughly comparable activities leading to roughly comparable states, even while the conceptual traditions in which they arose were quite diverse.

5.9.1   The day of a Jaina monk

I shall declare the correct behaviour which causes freedom from all misery; by practising it the Jaina monks have crossed the ocean of births and deaths . . .

After sunrise during the first quarter of the first quarter of the day he should inspect (and clean) his things and pay his respects to the superior.

Then, with his hands joined he should ask him : 'What shall I do now? I want to be employed, sir, in doing some work or in studying.'

If he is ordered to do some work, he should do it without tiring; if he is ordered to study, he should do it without allowing himself to be affected by any pains.

A clever monk should divide the day into four (equal) parts, and fulfil his duties in all four parts.

In the first quarter he should study, in the second he should meditate, in the third he should go on his begging-tour, and in the fourth he should study again . . .

A clever monk should divide the night too into four parts, and fulfil his duties in all four parts.

In the first quarter he should study, in the second he should meditate, in the third he should leave off sleep, and in the fourth he should study again . . .

In the last quarter of the first quarter of the day, after paying his respect to the Guru, a monk should inspect his almsbowl . . .

He should first inspect his mouth-cloth, then his broom . . .
Jacobi, *Jaina Sutras Part II,* 142-5

The passage is edited to avoid numerous technical terms. The mouth-cloth and broom are accessories used to avoid harming living beings. Cf 3.2.5.

5.9.2 The day of a Zen monk

The most urgent task is to study and master Zen. Therefore, whenever you have a view to discuss with the master, consult with the directing monk (*jikijitsu*) and try to see the master regardless of the hours of the day . . .

During the meditation hours, no one is permitted to leave the Hall, except for interviewing the master. To other necessary movements, the intermission hours are to be devoted. While outside, no whispering, no tarrying is allowed . . .

At the time of the tea-ceremony (*sarei*) taking place twice a day, no one shall be absent; no left-overs are to be thrown on the floor . . .

At the time of morning service, the dozing ones are to be severely dealt with the *keisaku* (warning stick).

At meal-time the monks are to conduct themselves quietly and to make no noise in the handling of the bowls; the waiting monks should move about quietly and in due decorum.

When the meditation hours are over at night, go right to bed; do not disturb others by sutra-reading, or bowings, or whispering with the neighbouring monks . . .

When the monks go out for their begging round, they are not to swing their arms, or put their hands inside the dress, or walk the streets staggeringly, or whisper to one another; for such behaviours are damaging to the dignity of monkhood . . . Suzuki. *The Training of the Zen Buddhist Monk,* 148-150

5.10 STATES, ACTION AND CONCEPTS

These may be related in various ways which cut across the possible social shapes of religion. For example, the subject of an experience of the 'numinous' (cf 3.3) may be a religious specialist in a simple group or civil religion. On the other hand he may be a member of a minor group religion quite distinct from established orthodoxy. He may even be involved quite casually and incidentally in some unexpected way (folk religion).

5.10.1   Isaiah in the temple

In the year that King Uzzi'ah died I saw the Lord sitting upon a throne, high and lifted up; and his train filled the temple. Above him stood the seraphim; each had six wings : with two he covered his face, and with two he covered his feet, and with two he flew. And one called to another and said :

> 'Holy, holy, holy is the LORD of hosts;
> the whole earth is full of his glory.'

And the foundations of the thresholds shook at the voice of him who called, and the house was filled with smoke. And I said : 'Woe is me! For I am lost; for I am a man of unclean lips, and I dwell in the midst of a people of unclean lips; for my eyes have seen the King, the LORD of hosts!'

Then flew one of the seraphim to me, having in his hand a burning coal which he had taken with tongs from the altar. And he touched my mouth, and said : 'Behold, this has touched your lips; your guilt is taken away, and your sin forgiven.' And I heard the voice of the Lord saying, 'Whom shall I send, and who will go for us?' Then I said, 'Here am I! Send me.' Isaiah vi, 1-8

5.10.2   Joseph Smith in the woods

According to previous arrangement, I commenced by vocal prayer to our Heavenly Father, and was followed by each of the others in succession. We did not at the first trial, however, obtain any answer or manifestation of divine favour in our behalf. We again observed the same order of prayer, each calling on and praying fervently to God in rotation, but with the same result as before.

Upon this, our second failure, Martin Harris proposed that he should withdraw himself from us, believing as he expressed himself, that his presence was the cause of our not obtaining what we wished for. He accordingly withdrew from us, and we knelt down again, and had not been many minutes engaged in prayer, when presently we beheld a light above us in the air of exceeding brightness; and behold an angel stood before us. In his hands he held the plates . . . He turned over the leaves one by one, so that we could see them, and discern the engravings thereon distinctly. He then addressed himself to David Whitmer, and said, 'David, blessed is the Lord, and he that keeps his commandments'; when, immediately afterwards, we heard a voice from out of the bright light above us, saying, 'These plates have been revealed by the power of God, and they have been translated by the power of God. The translation of them which you have seen is correct, and I command you to bear record of what you now see and hear.' Joseph Smith. *Joseph Smith's Testimony* (pamphlet published by The Church of Jesus Christ of Latter-day Saints, no date), 23-4

5.10.3 The ghost by the fishpond

One night a member of the guard was sleeping in the fishing pavilion by the large pool when about midnight he felt his face being gently stroked by a skinny hand. His flesh creeping with horror, the man drew his sword, and with his other hand, grabbed what turned out to be an extraordinarily wretched-looking old man dressed in a pale blue coat and trousers. 'I once owned this place and lived here,' said the old man. 'I am the younger brother of Urashima Tarō. I have lived here since ancient times, for more than twelve hundred years. I beg you to let me go, and build a shrine here for me. If you do, I will do all I can to protect you.' 'This is not a matter I can decide by myself,' said the guard. 'I shall have to inform His Majesty the Retired Emperor first.' 'Damn you for refusing!' shouted the ghost, and kicked the man up into the air three times, till he was limp and battered to a pulp, then as he fell to the ground, the ghost opened its mouth and swallowed him up. The old man had seemed just an average size, but he turned into such an enormous ghost that he ate the man at a single gulp. D. E. Mills (trans). *A Collection of Tales from Uji* (Cambridge 1970), 376

5.11   ALL FOUR ASPECTS

In each of the cases below the state of mind engendered in the religious group may be seen to have had an effect on certain lines of religious thought and action. The incidentally contributive factors of threatened persecution and the unexpected death of the Foundress, in the Tenrikyo case, may be counterbalanced in the Christian case by the unplanned persistent presence of Gentiles.

5.11.1   Even the Gentiles

Peter was still speaking when the Holy Spirit came upon all who were listening to the message. The believers who had come with Peter, men of Jewish birth, were astonished that the gift of the Holy Spirit should have been poured out even on Gentiles. For they could hear them speaking in tongues of ecstasy and acclaiming the greatness of God. Then Peter spoke : 'Is anyone prepared to withhold the water for baptism from these persons, who have received the Holy Spirit just as we did ourselves?' Then he ordered them to be baptised in the name of Jesus Christ. After that they asked him to stay on with them for a time.

News came to the apostles and the members of the church in Judaea that Gentiles too had accepted the word of God; and when Peter came up to Jerusalem those who were of Jewish birth raised the question with him. 'You have been visiting men who are uncircumcised,' they said, 'and sitting at table with them !' Peter began by laying before them the facts as they had happened. Acts x, 44 – xi, 4

5.11.2 The death of a foundress

Her [the Foundress'] condition was becoming more serious. Then the attendants, making up their minds to perform the service, set themselves to its preparation and after providing against every possible emergency, they began publicly to perform the service to the accompaniment of musical instruments including a drum, around one o'clock in the afternoon. That day there were so many worshippers that the bamboo palisades set up on the east and south sides of the Kanrōdai were broken to pieces. But no policeman came to the scene till the last. It must be surely because God the Parent had accepted the sincerity of the people and shown His wonderful providence. Thus successfully having performed the service and coming back to their room from the Kanrōdai, they heard the news of her ascension. At the news they burst out crying, but soon sank into silence. In the silence of sad grief they spent half an hour, and an hour, with folded arms and bent heads. By and by plucking up their courage, they again asked Izō Iburi about the divine will concerning the ascension of the Foundress in the upstair room of the storehouse, and were replied, 'Loving my children so much, I have decided to shorten My natural term of physical existence by twenty-five years and start out to save the world . . .'

In short, for the purpose of hastening the universal saving of man, the Foundress receded from Her physical appearance. Consequently, Her departure is not considered to be the end of Her life and mission but the beginning of the divine saving work beyond the limitation of Her physical existence. Tenrikyo Kyokai Honbu. *A Short History of Tenrikyo*, 89 and 92

The natural term of life is supposed to be 115 years except as shortened by 'dust' or karma, from which the Foundress was believed free. Izō Iburi was the leading follower of the Foundress, who died in 1887, and then the main organiser of the religion which spread rapidly thereafter.

PART SIX

Religion and General Social Factors

An approach to the relationship between religion and general social factors was made above in the Introduction (pp. 17ff). It was argued that attempts to achieve total definitive explanations should be relegated to the wider field of discussion termed 'further questions'. The search for specific relationships between religion and other social factors however is one of the proper tasks of the sociology of religion, and a proper extension of the comparative study of religion.

The possibly various manner of these relationships has been stressed recently by Roland Robertson in his book *The Sociological Interpretation of Religion* (pp 59-60) where he writes, 'The only way out of such dilemmas appears to be that sociologists should regard as open the question of causal priorities in each specific case which they examine, rather than attempt to discover an ubiquitous and universal set of social processes which are productive of religious phenomena. This means that we should realise that in some social systems religion is a relatively independent variable and that in other social systems it is a relatively dependent variable. Thus religion at some time and in some place may be relatively autonomous and determinate with respect to other processes and structures within a social system and at other times and places it may be "at the mercy" of political, economic and other social factors.'

The extracts below briefly illustrate selected major topics in this area of 'explanation'. They also illustrate, especially in 6.4 and 6.5, that while the comparative study of religion inevitably leads us to seek explanations in the wider social context, the latter may also swing us back to a reconsideration of the intention of the religious phenomena themselves.

6.1 LEGITIMATION

It could be argued in a general way that all forms of simple group and civil religion (cf 2.1 and 2.2) serve to justify or legitimate the form of society in which they are found. After all they offer an integrated symbolic mirror reflecting the presumed proper order of things. This line of interpretation is particularly associated with Durkheim's account of religion. However the legitimation of quite specific aspects of social action such as military action (cf 1.10.3) or economic policies (cf 6.4) is much more readily illustrated. At this level what is meant is that the religious datum is correlated with a social state of affairs which is otherwise considered desirable and which is perhaps not altogether achieved; hence the religious ideas seem to be harnessed in support. The persons involved do not see it self-consciously as a legitimation, but rather as a simple inner rapport between beliefs and situation. Elementary illustrations follow.

6.1.1 Piety is useful to states

I propose that *there shall be shrines in cities,* on this point not following the Persian Magi, in accordance with whose advice Xerxes is said to have burned the temples of Greece on the ground that the Greeks shut up the gods within walls, whereas all places consecrated to them ought to be open and free, seeing that this whole universe is their temple and home. The Greeks and Romans have done a better thing : for it has been our wish, to the end that we may promote piety towards the gods, that they should dwell in our cities with us. For this idea encourages a religious attitude that is useful to States (*civitatibus*) . . . *The groves in the country* have the same purpose. Nor is the worship of the *Lares,* handed down by our ancestors, established in sight of farm and homestead, and shared by slaves as well as masters, to be rejected. Marcus Tullius Cicero. (C. W. Keyes trans). *De Re Publica, De Legibus* (1928), 403 (Laws II, x-xi)

6.1.2   An awful warning

When, therefore, Julian set himself against the Most High, his daring was vain, as it was impious . . . A slave of ambition, which no power could satiate; a mover of cruelty, which no innocence could disarm; and a boaster of impiety, which no mercies, however signal, however renewed, could either alarm or overcome —in the prime of manhood; at the height of his fame; in the hour of victory—with all his wisdom, all his power, all his soul arrayed against God—the wounded apostate dies !

What an awful warning to those who are active for evil ! What a lesson to us all, to be humble and contented in our station ! Surely the Christian could nowhere be found, who would change his lowliest lot for that of the imperial and apostate Julian ! James. *A Comment upon the Collects,* 381-2

The Emperor Julian lived between 331 and 363. Needless to say there is no inherent connection between Julian's short-lived attempt to reverse the Christianisation of the Roman Empire and any dissatisfaction people may have felt with the class structure of Victorian England (when this comment was made).

6.1.3   America needs this pamphlet

AMERICA NEEDS THIS PAMPHLET !

The 24-page Book, 'War in Vietnam : Should Christians

fight ?' Is the Bible Answer to All the Communists, the Pacifists, the Liberals in Church and Government, the Unpatriotic Rebels Against the Government and Beatniks Who Burn Draft Cards . . .

Here are subheads from the book :

I. No One, Acting for Himself, Has a Right to Kill
II. But God Himself Kills
III. God Authorises Governments to Kill Criminals
IV. God Sometimes Justifies a Nation's Going to War
V. Then Good Christians Should Obey the Government When Young Men Are Drafted for the War in Vietnam or Protection of American Homeland
VI. Christians Should Pray for Wars to Cease

America needs this pamphlet. You may have it absolutely free if you write during April and request it.

John R. Rice (ed). *The Sword of the Lord, An Independent Christian Weekly, Standing for the Verbal Inspiration of the Bible, the Deity of Christ, His Blood Atonement, Salvation by Faith, New Testament Soul Winning and the Premillennial Return of Christ. Opposes Modernism, Worldliness and Formalism.* (Murfreesboro, Tennessee, 15 April 1966), 6

6.1.4 White minorities have rights, too
White Minorities Have Rights, Too.

We believe, as do other intelligent, well-meaning Christian people, that as citizens Negroes ought to have the same rights that others enjoy, the right for an education, the right to vote, the right to protection of the laws. However, the rest of the world has rights, too, and they are just as important as the rights of coloured people . . .

There is a text of scripture that good Christian people ought to carefully consider here : 'Thou shalt not follow a multitude to do evil; neither shalt thou speak in a cause to decline after many to wrest judgement : Neither shalt thou countenance a poor man in his cause' (Exod 23 :2, 3). It is wrong to follow the crowd in a popular movement that ignores the rights of others and tends to lawbreaking. To do wrong in the cause of a poor man is just as wicked as to do wrong in the cause of a rich man. To take the part of a poor man or an ignorant man or a Negro man because he is poor or perhaps because he has suffered more, without fair, impartial judgement, is a sin.

Mob rule is always wrong, and the present New Deal, social-istic, Democratic administration of President Johnson tends to take the money from those who earn it to give it to those who do not, tends to ignore the rights of non-union people to keep the votes of the labour union crowd, tends to ignore the rights of white minorities in order to gain the votes of the organised and unified Negroes. Those who 'follow a multitude to do evil' sin against God, even though they do have the majority with them. Rice. *The Sword of the Lord* (3 September 1965), 1 and (cont) 8

Cf previous extract. Religion may be used to justify resistance to government policy as well as obedience to it.

6.1.5   Men are in charge of women
Men are in charge of women, because Allah hath made one of them to excel the other, and because they spend of their property (for the support of women). So good women are the obedient, guarding in secret that which Allah hath guarded. As for those from whom ye fear rebellion, admonish them and banish them to beds apart, and scourge them. Then if they obey you, seek not a way against them. Lo! Allah is ever High Exalted, Great. Pickthall. *The Meaning of the Glorious Koran*, 83 (Sūrah iv, 34)

6.2   SOCIAL CRISIS AND CHANGE
It would be a mistake to think of religion merely as a kind of compensating fluid which operated to maintain equilibrium when other aspects of society temporarily fail to harmonise 'properly'. Religion is just as often the occasion or the accom-

paniment of social crisis and change. Vittorio Lanternari, in
The Religions of the Oppressed (1965), has catalogued just
such a type of religion which appeared in the context of the
confrontation of technologically advanced western society
with peasant or other simple communities across the world.
Similarly, other religions offer real status and prosperity to relatively deprived groups; others are revolutionary movements
which seek ultimately to change society as a whole; yet others
are specialised utopian communities whose members withdraw
from society at large and offer a minority alternative to general
social change.

6.2.1   The Ras Tafari movement

The religious services held Sunday evenings begin with singing
and are usually followed by this dialogue between the preacher
and the congregation :

Speaker : How did we get here ?

People : Slavery.

Speaker : Who brought us from Ethiopia ?

People : The white man.

Speaker : The white man tells us we are inferior, but we are
not inferior. We are superior and he is inferior. The time has
come for us to go home. In the near future we shall go back to
Ethiopia and the white man shall be our servant. The white man
says we are no good, yet David, Solomon, and the Queen of
Sheba were black. The English are criminals and the black
traitors [meaning the middle-class Jamaicans] are just as bad.
There is no freedom in Jamaica. The black man who does not
want to go back to Ethiopia doesn't want freedom. Ras Tafari
started Mau Mau. Ras Tafari says : Death to the White Man !

People : And to the Black Traitor ! We believe in one God,
one aim, one destiny. We believe in Africa for the Africans, at
home and abroad.

Vittoria Lanternari. *The Religions of the Oppressed* (New York
1965), 136 (quoting G. E. Simpson. 'Political Cultism in West

Kingston, Jamaica' *Social and Economic Studies* (Kingston, Jamaica) IV, 2 (1955), 135-6)

The Ras Tafari sects pay special reverence to the Emperor Hailie Selassie of Ethiopia who, it is believed, will one day recall them to the 'homeland', to which as ancient 'Israelite' tribes they belong.

6.2.2   Freedom from untouchability

A young Thai monk, now studying in Poona, said, 'I want the work of Dr Ambedkar to continue. Not so much to make them Buddhists, but to make them men, truly human.' . . . A young college student in Poona explained, 'We are not "less than men". But we could not be this in the caste system. We want a full life, to show we are intelligent, that our sons can learn . . . we want equality. We must be selfish to save ourselves; each must make progress for himself.' In Chikkhalwadi village, the people now 'have a different feeling'. They have discarded vicious habits (drink, bad language, fighting) and 'where before they felt inferiority and no ambition or energy to better their lot, now they have hope, and can advance. They no longer do the traditional mean jobs (as sweepers, removers of carrion, etc) and are no longer Untouchable, because of Buddhism.' . . . 'After conversion we feel we are no more Hindus, we are not Untouchable. It gives some sort of solace.' 'Buddhism is more revolutionary than Communism today. As Buddhists, we can walk anywhere with raised eyes.' M. Adele Fiske. 'Religion and Buddhism Among India's New Buddhists', *Social Research,* 36, no 1 (Spring 1969), 140-1

These comments refer to a conversion movement in which over three million of the former Untouchable Castes in India have become Buddhists, simultaneously achieving a new position in society. Dr Ambedkar was the leading personality, interpreting Buddhism in a rationalist, humanist and egalitarian manner. Many of those involved believe that they were 'originally'

Buddhists and are returning to the religion of their ancestors (cf 6.2.1).

6.2.3 Cargo cults

The millennium was to commence in two weeks, it was said. When that period expired, the Day was promised for another three weeks' time, and when that period ended without the ancestors having arrived, the event was postponed once more. It was expected that a steamer, the *Silubloan,* would arrive with the spirits of the dead, and would tie up at a jetty which was to rise up out of the sea at the western tip of Saibai. One man claimed that the steamer was coming from Canaan, but the *markai* [spirits of the dead] were to embark at a place called 'German town' in the far west. The vessel was to call at Thursday Island, where the *markai* would overcome and kill the Whites, and then proceed to Saibai.

Then would the cargo be dispensed . . . Peter Worsley. *The Trumpet Shall Sound, A Study of 'Cargo' Cults in Melanesia* (1957), 95-6

6.2.4 An alternative to ordinary life

Some may assert that this way of life goes against family ethics. But even in ordinary life there are few families all of whose members respect, believe in and love one another, even though on the surface they may appear to be living in harmony. There was nothing very wrong about my family in my old life, but the members lived in a false position when compared with my family in this new life. In my present family no member seeks to have his own way. Instead he surrenders himself to Light. More than twenty people have come from both north and south of Japan to stay in this house. Ittoen Tenko-san. *A New Road to Ancient Truth* (1969), 111

Tenko Nishida, otherwise known as Tenko-san or Ittoen Tenko-san, who lived from 1872 to 1968, founded a community known as Ittoen in which the emphasis is on going out to undertake menial and unpleasant tasks for other people (without payment, of course). No reliance whatever is placed on commercial activity or financial security. Cf 7.2.3.

6.2.5 Class struggles

The Communist League, an international association of workers, which could of course be only a secret one under the conditions obtaining at the time, commissioned the undersigned, at the Congress held in London in November 1847, to draw up for publication a detailed theoretical and practical programme of the Party . . .

The history of all hitherto existing society is the history of class struggles . . .

The Communists disdain to conceal their views and aims They openly declare that their ends can be attained only by the forcible overthrow of all existing social conditions. Let the ruling classes tremble at a Communistic revolution. The proletarians have nothing to lose but their chains. They have a world to win.

WORKING MEN OF ALL COUNTRIES, UNITE!

K. Marx and F. Engels. *Manifesto of the Communist Party* (Moscow 1952), 7 (Preface to the German edition of 1872), 39 (opening sentence), and 94

The original German text was published in 1848.

6.3 URBANISATION AND SECULARISATION

Urbanisation and secularisation are both processes which involve the fossilisation or dismantling of existing forms of religion. Urbanisation is not a new phenomenon, but it has been especially widespread and rapid in modern times. It has led to the relative loss of influence on the part of traditional religions, though not necessarily of religion altogether, as the emergence of different or new religions has shown, especially in Japan and America and to some extent in Europe. The term 'secularisation' implies rather more, since it means the

N

passing of domains hitherto considered 'holy' into the sphere of 'ordinary' life. This has frequently meant both the conscious, political disestablishment of religious institutions and also the intellectual disestablishment of religious ways of thought, though neither of these *necessarily* implies the other.

6.3.1 Cicero tames the gods

It is a good thing also that *Intellect, Piety, Virtue and Good Faith should be arbitrarily deified;* and in Rome temples have been dedicated by the State to all these qualities, the purpose being that those who possess them (and all good men do) should believe that the gods themselves are established within their own souls . . . for it is proper to deify the virtues *but not the vices.* The ancient altar to Fever on the Palatine and the one to Bad Fortune on the Esquiline as well as all other abominations of that character must be done away with. But if we must invent names for the gods, we ought rather to choose such titles as Vica Pota, derived from Victory and Power, and Stata, from the idea of standing firm, and such epithets as those of the Strengthener and the Invincible, which are given to Jupiter; also the names of things which we should desire, such as Safety, Honour, Wealth and Victory. Cicero. *De Legibus*, 405 (Laws II, xi)

Although Cicero saw religion as playing an important role in the State (cf 6.1.1) his fundamental line of thought is that it is not the gods that matter, but men; hence his patronising, managerial, and at bottom desacralising approach.

6.3.2 Buddhist urban temples

The nucleus of the connections between the temple and the citizens in general is formed by the temple-supporter relationship. But this relationship does not reveal itself clearly in aspects other than funeral and memorial services for the respose of the ancestral souls.

The percentage of those among the Buddhist temples which

have affiliated facilities amounts to 14.9% in Tokyo and 5.1% in Osaka. Most of these facilities consist of kindergarten or nursery. All of them claim to aim primarily at giving religious education, but they are being utilised at the same time as a means of establishing a stable temple economy . . .

The chief priests having a side job amount to 26.9% in Tokyo and 19.9% in Osaka. The side jobs consist mostly of teaching profession and government (local as well as national) service. Although this derives from the weak foundation of the temple economy, the preoccupation with the side job has resulted in making the temple activities more passive than ever, in weakening the temple-supporter relationship, and in deepening the gap between the temple and society in general . . .

It may be added in passing that the visitors to the temples' festivals (ennichi) included a considerable number of people who made the visit for recreational purposes that had absolutely nothing or almost nothing to do with religious faith. This suggests that the institution of 'ennichi', which originally was a temple function, is gradually being severed from religion in contemporary society. Kawasaki, Kashigumi and Masuda. *Toshijiin no Shakaiteki Kino* (ie 'The Social Functions of Urban Temples') Vol I (Tokyo 1959), 142-3 ('Summary of the Results' in English)

6.3.3   Education and secularisation

The situation was entirely different in the past when most people were not educated and when church and chapel provided the only channel of popular instruction. But today, when the whole population of every civilised country is subjected to an intensive process of schooling during the most impressionable years of their lives, it is the school and not the church that forms men's minds, and if the school finds no place for religion, there will be no room left for religion elsewhere. It is no accident that the introduction of universal compulsory state education has coincided in time and place with the secularisation of modern culture . . .

The trouble is that our modern secular cuture is sub-literary
as well as sub-religious. The forces that affect it are in the West
the great commercialised amusement industries . . . Christopher
Dawson. *The Historic Reality of Christian Culture* (New York
1960), 87-9

While Christian theologians broadly agree on the facts of secularisation, they do not all agree on their meaning and value.
Contrast for example *The Secular City* (1965) by Harvey Cox,
in which many modern trends are welcomed.

6.3.4 Throwing away the portraits

Q. Now that the lights are on, the green floor, the portrait of the
Empress of Heaven and the Earth God on the floor look especially nice. Do the portrait and the Earth God have any significant
meaning to you?

A. They no longer have any significant meaning. We put
them here just because we used to have them in the country. I
think it is mere superstition.

Q. If you think this is superstition, you can stop worshipping
them, can't you?

A. Oh, it doesn't matter.

Q. What do you mean by this? Do you mean you don't have
to worship?

A. It really does not matter.

Q. Are the portrait of the Empress of Heaven and the shrine
of the Earth God the same as in your country home?

A. No, we threw them away when we moved here. These are
new ones.

Q. Do you have to follow any rites when you throw away the
old ones? Is there anything you must avoid doing?

A. No, we simply throw them away.

Berkowitz, Brandauer and Reed, 'Folk Religion in an Urban

Setting, A Study of Hakka Villagers in Transition', 86-7

6.4 RELIGION AND ECONOMICS

There does not seem to be any simple correlation between economic situations and religious activity; that is, depression or prosperity do not seem to be associated per se with greater or less religious activity (cf Argyle, *Religious Behaviour*, 139), or for that matter with different kinds of religious activity. Relative deprivation has been mentioned above (6.2) as a possible occasion of religious movements, but this involves matters of status as well as of money. Dwindling financial resources are sometimes given as the motivation for the amalgamation of churches in the Ecumenical movement, but if this were a major factor here one might expect near-uniformity of religious belief and practice among the poor and lack of interest in ecclesiastical co-operation among the rich. Again, even though religious buildings to some extent reflect the relative wealth of their patrons, scales of values seem to be more important. For example, twentieth century Europe can hardly 'afford' to repair the cathedrals built in the middle ages. This is not to say that economics has no effect on religious behaviour at all (cf 6.3.2). Conversely we cannot assume that people's religious beliefs and attitudes have *no* effect on the world of business and economic affairs (*contra* Argyle, *Religious Behaviour*, 139), difficult though this may be to establish, let alone to measure. For example, if thrift is to be cherished except with regard to limited approved areas of expenditure (cf 6.4.5) or if pleasures and worldly commodities are not to be sought (cf 6.4.6), the 'blessings of God' which accrue in return for labour as a businessman can only be saved and invested. It was along such lines that Max Weber argued in *The Protestant Ethic and the Spirit of Capitalism* (English, 1930), thus giving rise to a sustained discussion of the role of religion in this important area. The extracts given below show religion establishing the framework of integrity without which commerce is impossible; religious attitudes possibly having an effect on patterns of economic activity; and religion as the legitimation of particular economic policies.

6.4.1 Fair dealing in Babylon

What is he benefited who invests money in unscrupulous
    trading?
He is disappointed in the matter of profit and loses his capital.
He who invests money in distant trading missions and pays one
    shekel per . . .
It is pleasing to Shamash, and he will prolong his life.
The merchant who [practises] trickery as he holds the balances,
    who uses two sets of weights . . .
He is disappointed in the matter of profit and loses his
    capital . . .
The honest merchant who weighs out loans [of corn] by the
    [maxi]mum standard, thus multiplying kindness,
It is pleasing to Shamash, and he will prolong his life,
He will enlarge his family, gain wealth,
And like the water of a never failing spring [his] descendants
    will never fail.
D. Winton Thomas (ed). *Documents From Old Testament Times* (1958), 109

Shamash was the Mesopotamian sun-god and god of justice.

6.4.2 Neo-Confucian rules for merchant seamen

Commerce is the business of selling and buying in order to bring profit to both parties. It is not to gain profit at the expense of others. When profit is shared the gain may be large but the benefits are small. 'Profit is the happy outcome of righteousness.' So while the greedy merchant bids for five, the decent one bids for three. Keep that in mind.

    Foreign lands may differ from our own in manners and speech, but as to the nature bestowed upon men by heaven there cannot be any difference . . . Heaven does not tolerate deception. Be mindful, therefore, not to bring disgrace upon our country's tradition. Tsunoda. *Sources of Japanese Tradition,* 349 (quoting *Fujiwara Seika shū* I, 126-7)

Fujiwara Seika was instrumental in establishing Neo-Confucianism as the state orthodoxy of seventeenth century Japan, and these rules were drawn up in connection with a trading mission to Annam. Tsunoda notes 'the characteristic Confucian subordination of the profit motive to equity and mutual benefit'.

6.4.3   Calvin on interest

I have, then, admonished men that the fact itself is simply to be considered that all unjust gains are ever displeasing to God, whatever colour we endeavour to give to it. But if we would form an equitable judgement, reason does not suffer us to admit that all usury is to be condemned without exception. If the debtor has protracted the time by false pretences to the loss and inconvenience of his creditor, will it be consistent that he should reap advantage from his bad faith and broken promises? Certainly, no one, I think, will deny that usury ought to be paid to the creditor in addition to the principal, to compensate his loss. If any rich and monied man, wishing to buy a piece of land, should borrow some part of the sum required of another, may not he who lends the money receive some part of the revenues of the farm until the principal shall be repaid? Many such cases daily occur in which, as far as equity is concerned, usury is no worse than purchase . . . But those who think differently may object, that we must abide by God's judgement, when he generally prohibits usury to his people. I reply, that the question is only as to the poor, and consequently, if we have to do with the rich, that usury is freely permitted . . . M. J. Kitch. *Capitalism and the Reformation* (1967), 130 (quoting C. W. Bingham (trans). *Commentaries on the Four Last Books of Moses* (1852), 150-1)

For the Biblical prohibition of taking interest from the poor, cf Leviticus xxv, 35-7. Kitch points out that Calvin was 'the first theologian to deny that usury per se was contrary to the word of God', and that this marked an important stage in the development of protestant attitudes.

6.4.4 The Way of the merchant

Obtaining profit from sale is the Way of the merchant. I have not heard selling at cost called the Way . . . The merchant's profit from sale is like the *samurai*'s stipend. No profit from sale would be like the *samurai* serving without a stipend . . .

When one says 'the way of the merchant' how can it differ from the way of the *samurai,* farmer or artisan? Mencius said, there is only one way. *Samurai,* farmer, artisan and merchant are each creatures of heaven. In heaven are there two ways? Robert N. Bellah. *Tokugawa Religion, The Values of Pre-Industrial Japan* (New York 1957), 161 and 160 (quoting the *Toimondō* of Baigan Ishida)

Ishida (1685-1744) began a religious and ethical movement which offered a dignified and disciplined way of life for the hitherto rather despised merchant class of Tokugawa Japan.

6.4.5 Seven principles

1. Revere Shintoism, Buddhism and Confucianism and cherish sincerity in all.

2. Obey the law, accept your social position and cherish thrift.

3. Make your household harmonious and cherish your trade, your calling.

4. Cherish loyalty, filial piety and forbearance.

5. Cherish compassion, secret charity, caring for one's body and caring for one's family.

6. Make your conduct good and cherish the education of children and retainers.

7.   Know that blessings are to be found in work and cherish your work of today.

Bellah. *Tokugawa Religion,* 173

These admonitions from a later follower of Baigan Ishida (cf 6.4.4), current in the early nineteenth century, may be compared with the emphasis on proper occupation, diligence and thrift associated with the 'protestant ethic' in Europe and America (cf 6.4.6).

6.4.6 Diligence and its rewards

A vocation or calling is a certain kind of life, ordained and imposed on man by God, for the common good. First of all, I say, it is a certain condition or kind of life : that is, a certain manner of leading our lives in this world . . .

They profane their lives and Callings that employ them to get honours, pleasures, profits, worldly commodities, etc. for thus we live to another end than God hath appointed, and there we serve ourselves, and consequently neither God nor man . . . The true end of our lives is, to do service to God, in serving of man : and for a recompense of this service God sends his blessings on men's travails, and he allows them to take for their labours . . .

The second overall rule which must be remembered, is this : that every man must do the duty of his Calling with diligence . . . Of this diligence there be two reasons : first of all, the end why God bestows his gifts upon us, is, that they might be employed in his service, and to his glory . . . Secondly, to them which employ their gifts, more is given . . . Kitch. *Capitalism and the Reformation,* 153-4 (quoting William Perkins' 'Treatise on Vocation or Calling of Men' in *Works* (1626), vol 1, 750-60)

6.4.7 The moral principles of wage restraint

Sir Frederick vouched for the support many people would give if the Church would preach Christian principles. He outlined these as :

1. 'We should love our neighbour as ourself, and no section of society should exploit its economic power to its neighbour's hurt.'

2. 'The strong should help the weak.'

3. 'Those capable of working should help those who are not.'

4. 'No one should be unemployed.'

5. 'That we are forbidden to covet.'

Self discipline not to covet meant, among other things, forgoing differentials for the general good. Every time there was an attempt to get justice for one group of workers there was a move by militants to restore the differential.

Sir Frederick said that if the Church would preach such principles loud and clear, it would 'strike a chord in the consciences of sufficient people to make a rational, just, prices and incomes policy feasible.'

As a result—'as should happen when a nation follows Christian principles'—the country would be a good deal better off both spiritually and materially.

He also asked management to consider the parable of the talents. If management was dedicated to turning its two talents into four and its five into ten, productivity would rise at a far higher rate and inflation would be a good deal less.

The Archbishop of Canterbury, Dr Ramsey, described the session as 'memorable.' *Guardian*, 28 April 1971

6.5 SOCIAL NEEDS AND RELIGIOUS MEANINGS

Minor group religions with a critical stance towards the world at large (cf 5.6) normally have two main types of rite, initiatory and intensifying (cf 5.7). As such religions develop a broader social base they tend to develop also those rites of transition which are everywhere required, especially those connected with birth (cf 1.8), adolescence (cf 5.3), marriage and death. Less obvious is the fact that such rites, which have on the one hand a common human meaning, may also be transcended from within by the specific meanings of the minor group religion whose services are offered. The expansion of a religious system in these directions may therefore be viewed in two ways: sociologically, as a response to universal social

needs, and phenomenologically, as an opportunity for routinised religious communication. Entered below are first of all a
funeral which is a more or less straightforward social occasion,
and then by contrast two examples which are shot through
with soteriological motifs.

6.5.1 Beowulf's funeral

The people of the Geats prepared for Beowulf, as he had asked
of them, a splendid pyre hung about with helmets, shields, and
shining corselets. Then, mourning, the soldiers laid their loved
and illustrious prince in the midst. Upon the hill the men-at-
arms lit a gigantic funeral fire. Black wood-smoke whirled over
the conflagration; the roar of flames mixed with the noise of
weeping, until the furious draught subsided and the white-hot
body crumbled to pieces. Sadly they complained of their grief
and of the death of their king. A Geat woman with braided hair
keened a dirge in Beowulf's memory, repeating again and
again that she feared bad times were on the way, with blood-
shed, terror, captivity, and shame. Heaven swallowed up the
smoke.

Upon the headland the Geats erected a broad, high tumulus,
plainly visible to distant seamen. In ten days they completed the
building of the hero's beacon. Round his ashes they built the
finest vault that their most skilful men could devise. Within the
barrow they placed collars, brooches, and all the trappings which
they had plundered from the treasure-hoard. They buried the
gold and left that princely treasure to the keeping of earth,
where it yet remains, as useless to men as it was before. Wright
Beowulf, 100-1

6.5.2 Buddhist funerals

If monks simply recited buddha's name, it was considered to
give rise to merit. Therefore, after someone died, they might be
asked to recite buddha's name for a week and then transfer the
resulting merit to his account. They might also be asked to chant

sutras, which not only gave rise to merit, but constituted a form of instruction. The soul of the deceased would be summoned to his tablet (and attracted by offerings) to hear the *Ksitigarbha Sutra* or the *Diamond Sutra* or the *Amitabha Sutra*. The latter was particularly effective in turning his mind toward the Western Paradise, where it was hoped he would be reborn.

All the rites described above were called 'Buddhist services' (*fo-shih* or *ching-ch'an*). They would be performed according to a schedule that varied with the wealth and piety of the bereaved and with the customs of the region. If a family could afford it they were performed day and night : otherwise on the third, fifth and seventh days after death and on several of the seven 'sevenths' during the first forty-nine days. Holmes Welch. *The Practice of Chinese Buddhism 1900-1950* (Cambridge, Mass. 1967), 188-9

6.5.3   Collect at the burial of the dead

O merciful God, the Father of our Lord Jesus Christ, who is the resurrection and the life; in whom whosoever believeth shall live, though he die; and whosoever liveth, and believeth in him, shall not die eternally; who also hath taught us, by his holy Apostle Saint Paul, not to be sorry, as men without hope, for them that sleep in him; We meekly beseech the, O Father, to raise us from the death of sin unto the life of righteousness; that, when we shall depart this life, we may rest in him, as our hope is this our *brother* doth; and that, at the general Resurrection in the last day, we may be found acceptable in thy sight; and receive that blessing, which thy well-beloved Son shall then pronounce to all that love and fear thee, saying, Come, ye blessed children of my Father, receive the kingdom prepared for you from the beginning of the world : Grant this, we beseech thee, O merciful Father, through Jesus Christ, our Mediator and Redeemer. Amen. *Book of Common Prayer,* from 'The Order of the Burial of the Dead'

6.5.4 Against compulsory baptism

Gradually the presbytery finds the courage to introduce carefully considered baptismal rules. In the case of parents who do not share in the life of the parish, the baptism of the children is postponed. However the child-blessing ceremony is offered to them as a diaconic-missionary service of the parish. In this way baptismal discipline is possible without discrimination. A special Church register is started for the blessings and the parents receive a certificate stating that the child-blessing has taken place. Gradually the socially compulsory character of infant baptism is dismantled and child-blessing and infant baptism come to be seen more and more as genuine alternatives. Hermann Wilkens. 'Kindersegnung oder Säuglingstaufe?' *Stimme der Gemeinde* 15 March 1971, 92

Dissatisfaction with the role of Christian baptism as a mere postnatal rite of transition led to the development of this alternative. The new system attempts to answer the social needs while maintaining the special meaning of Christian baptism. The extract offers indirect evidence of the social pressure as well as direct evidence of the response.

PART SEVEN

Religion and General Psychological Factors

The psychology of religion is in a state of some confusion, not least because there are various conflicting approaches among psychologists towards the study of psychology itself. The variety of topics which *could* be considered under this heading is amply illustrated in G. Stephens Spinks' survey *Psychology and Religion* (1963), but four only are raised below. Three are concerned with the development and maturity of the individual, and the fourth is about the effect which matters of general psychological importance may have upon the formulation of religious concepts. As in the case of the sources given for 'Religion and General Social Factors' above, it has not been possible to give a detailed experimental or statistical base. That would demand a specialised study of each topic going far beyond the scope required here, and various studies of this kind have been summarised in Michael Argyle's very useful *Religious Behaviour* (1958). Nevertheless it is hoped that the extracts given below illustrate the *kind* of question which is raised in correlative studies. In general, the suggestion is that the psychological factors more or less directly indicated have some formative or conditioning influence on the religious phenomena and hence are to some extent 'explanatory' of them, in the limited sense explained above (Introduction, pp 17ff).

Other similar topics which might have been considered here

are the relationship between religion and mental illness of various kinds (cf Argyle, 101-28), and sexual difference and sexual activity (cf Argyle, 71-9 and 121-8). Various writers, including Adorno, Eysenck, Ferguson and Fromm, have also attempted to correlate religious attitudes with 'authoritarian' and 'humanitarian' personality traits (cf Argyle's general discussion of differences in personality traits, 80-100). Nevertheless although there are of course some correlations to be made here, the results of studies made so far are mainly statistical and not easy to express in terms of source material. Moreover there seems to be little comparative basis for most of these studies, and hence there may be a danger of circularity; ie after complex analyses the investigators come to the startling conclusion that the attitudes of the subjects tend to fit in with their beliefs.

Another topic not considered below is the question about whether certain psychological 'types' can be correlated with specific types of religion. For example, just as James had distinguished between the 'healthy-minded' and the 'sick' soul (*Varieties of Religious Experience*, 77-162), so Sheldon distinguished between the 'viscerotonic', 'somatotonic' and 'cerebrotonic' (*The Varieties of Temperament*, New York 1942), and correlated various religious preferences with these. Such type theories however, which are different from the analysis of more specific personality traits in that they refer to whole individuals, have not achieved a very high degree of stability in the field of psychology in general and hence cannot be used reliably in correlative studies. As Stagner says, 'Each type theory represents the special interest of its inventor' (*Psychology of Personality* (New York 1965), 286).

Finally no attempt has been made to correlate religious belief and behaviour precisely with subconscious processes such as repression and sublimation as this could only be done by a highly specialised expert, if at all. That subconscious processes are important is widely accepted, for example, minimally, by Starbuck in his discussion of conversion (*The Psychology of Religion*, 101-17). The nearest approach below to the role of subconscious elements is in 7.4 (cf further discussion there), where psychological facts such as are commonly recognised to be important in depth psychology are presumed to impinge significantly on religion, and to emerge into consciousness in religious contexts.

7.1 MENTAL DEVELOPMENT AND RELIGIOUS THOUGHT

The Swiss psychologist Jean Piaget has defined three main stages in the development of thinking processes, namely: intuitive thought, concrete operational thought and abstract thought (cf *The Psychology of Intelligence,* 1950, or, for a brief account and wider bibliography, Nathan Isaacs' *The Growth of Understanding in the Young Child,* 1961); and this analysis has been applied to the religious development of children, in the Christian tradition, by Ronald Goldman in *Religious Thinking from Childhood to Adolescence* (1963). There are difficulties in relating Piaget's work to religious thinking, partly because people seem to vary more widely with regard to religion than they do with regard to their grasp of the volume of liquid in vessels of various sizes, and so on, but also because both expositors and critics have been writing at a time when there has been little agreement about the sense of theological language for adults. However, there may be some sense in distinguishing between religious language intended and understood in a concrete operational way, that is, graphic narrative or descriptive sequences assuming a cause and effect relationship between factors which are associated in terms of time and space, and religious language which conveys a meaning lying at one remove from the overt story form, that is to say, an abstract meaning. Frequently it is quite impossible to distinguish between these two ranges of meaning; indeed the same materials may bear both kinds of meaning at differ-

o

ent stages in the conceptual and religious development of the individual. Moreover, the second stage of thought may either be superseded as the individual develops or may persist as such. The fact that 'proof' of rebirth has been considered possible and significant by Buddhist apologists in modern times is perhaps a sufficient indication that the system of karma and rebirth illustrated below has been widely understood in a 'concrete operational' fashion. Yet, as is also illustrated, it is not always so understood. Similarly, the teaching of the ascension of Christ has at times been taken sufficiently literally for his 'absence' to be thought incompatible with his 'presence' in the Eucharist. Again, this also has been understood differently by others. Although these different kinds of understanding cannot be precisely identified with particular ages in the life of the individual, they do seem to demand different *mimimal* levels of mental development. (Cf 4.5.4-8).

7.1.1   Jaina hells

I shall now truly tell you another kind of perpetual suffering, how the sinners who have committed crimes suffer for the deeds they have done in their former lives.

Tying their hands and feet the (punishers) cut open their belly with razors and knives; taking hold of the mangled body of the sinner, they forcibly tear the skin off his back.

They cut off his arms at the armpits; they force his mouth wide open and scald it; they yoke the sinner to a car and drive him, and growing angry they pierce his back with a goad.

The (sinners) walk over ground burning and glowing like a red-hot iron; scorched they shriek horribly, being urged on with arrows and put to a red-hot yoke . . .

Whatever cruelty he has done in a former birth, the same will be inflicted on him in the Circle of Births. Having been born in an extremely miserable state of life, the sufferer experiences infinite pain.

A wise man hearing of these hells should not kill any living

being in the whole world; believing in true doctrines and renouncing all property he should know the world, but not become a slave to it.

Knowing the endless Circle of Births with regard to animals,
men, and gods, and the reward they will get; knowing all this,
(a wise man) should wait for his decease, practising meanwhile
self-control.

Thus I say.

Jacobi (trans). *Jaina Sutras*, Part II, 283 and 286 (from the
Sûtrakritânga I, 5, 2)

The hells are described in far greater elaboration than can be
quoted here, but the purpose of the elaboration is clearly stated
(cf 4.6.5).

7.1.2   Rebirth of a deva

When a deva falls from a company of devas,
Because his life is run, three sounds go forth
Of devas giving comfort : 'Go hence, friend,
To the happy bourn, to fellowship with men!
Becoming man, win faith incomparable
In dhamma true. That faith ingrained in thee
Rooted, stablished, in dhamma well proclaimed,
Shall not be rooted up while life doth last.
Leaving ill deeds of body, speech and mind,
And whatsoever else is deemed a sin,
Doing good deeds of body, speech and mind,
Of boundless merit, unattached thereto,
Then make the merit for thy future births
Greater by giving, and settle other mortals
In very dhamma, in the Brahma-life.'
Thus, when they know a deva is to fall,
They cheer him with these comfortable words,
And say : 'Come hither many times again.'

F. L. Woodward. *The Minor Anthologies of the Pali Canon*,
Part II (1948), 172 (*Itivuttaka: As It Was Said*, III, iv, iii)

A *deva* is one of the impermanent gods of Indian mythology, while *dhamma* here refers to the teaching of the Buddha.

7.1.3   Transmigration does not exist

Moreover, if one teaches that there is an end [to transmigration], it is only by placing oneself in worldly practice, from the point of view of worldly knowledge, with the purpose of encouraging beings fettered in the prison of transmigration. But if it is a question of what is real, transmigration itself does not exist. How then would it be destroyed? [That would be] like destroying the serpent [which is in reality a] rope, when one places it under the lamp. Jacques May (French trans). *Candrakīrti Prasanna-pactā Madhyamakavṛtti* (Paris 1959), 171

A rope may look like a serpent if one cannot see clearly.

7.1.4   Jesus departs and returns (i)

When he had said this, as they watched, he was lifted up, and a cloud removed him from their sight. As he was going, and as they were gazing intently into the sky, all at once there stood beside them two men in white who said, 'Men of Galilee, why stand there looking up into the sky? This Jesus, who has been taken away from you up to heaven, will come in the same way as you have seen him go.' Acts i, 9-11

It could perhaps be argued that the Gospel of Luke and the Acts of the Apostles together see 'salvation history' as a sequence of stages in which the Holy Spirit and Jesus are in turn present and absent. There is no 'mystical' presence of Jesus.

7.1.5   Jesus departs and returns (ii)

I will not leave you bereft; I am coming back to you. In a little while the world will see me no longer, but you will see me; because I live, you too will live; then you will know that I am in my Father, and you in me and I in you. John xiv, 18-20

7.2 ADOLESCENCE

'Conversion is a distinctively adolescent phenomenon', wrote Starbuck, claiming that it belongs almost exclusively to the years between ten and twenty-five (*The Psychology of Religion,* 28), and various later studies have confirmed this (cf Argyle, *Religious Behaviour,* 61). However it is possible to examine and write about teenage religion without considering the matter of 'conversion' at all, as H. Loukes did in *Teenage Religion* (1961). The quotations given from Loukes' investigation below display a range of belief and of scepticism, varying degrees of literalism, and attempts to correlate religious ideas with other knowledge and with experience of friendship and suffering. Various psychologists agree that dealing with such problems of meaning, or 'ideological adjustment' is a basic 'developmental task' of adolescence (cf Loukes, 104-5), whatever the prevailing religious beliefs or expectations may be at the time. Thus adolescence is a time of adjustment, of testing, and of *decision* (cf Argyle, 65), so that we might reformulate Starbuck's dictum to read 'Non-conversion or conversion are distinctively adolescent phenomena.' Of course the attainment of religious or other ideological standpoints in adolescence is linked to other matters such as the development of social and emotional maturity. Cf 3.1.

7.2.1 Adolescent conversions in Christianity

When 12 I had an impulse to go to the altar with two girl friends, but something kept me back. When 16, in a little meeting, I felt serious. My friend near me wanted me to go to the altar, and I thought on it and went.

When 12 or 13, at the advice of an old woman, I asked God to take my heart. I did feel very happy; I never have felt so sincere and earnest and anxious to be good. (Was confirmed at 16.)

I had made a start at 15 at revival meeting, but did not join church, and let it all pass over. (When 17) I felt the love and mercy of God. After an hour of pleading and prayer I felt relief from my sins.

I began to feel conviction at 11 years of age.
Starbuck. *The Psychology of Religion*, 46

Some of Starbuck's many cases. Cf 3.1.1.

7.2.2   Some adolescent thoughts on heaven
I think there is a heaven. Jesus said there was. If there isn't, then where do our souls go when we die?

I think there is a heaven, but you won't go there if you do not believe in Jesus Christ.

I believe there is a heaven. I don't think you stop in your grave for the rest of your life, and I don't think you come back to this earth but you have to go somewhere and I think heaven is where you go.

I believe in Jesus Christ so I *know* that I am going to heaven. As for the people who don't believe in Jesus Christ, I can also answer that. They will be going to hell.

I believe there is a heaven but not a hell.

I think there is a heaven, and I think God takes good and bad.

I think that there is a new world where everyone's happy and you always live there and meet everybody there again.

I believe that there is another world. I don't know where,

better and cleaner than our world. We are put on this earth to test us.

I think there is a place where you go after you have died, but I don't think it will be so wonderful as it is sometimes made out to be.

I do not think there is a heaven. I think we are just buried and that is where we stay.

I don't believe there is such a place as heaven. When you're dead you're dead. Some people preach there is a place called heaven—others say it is on earth—I don't care where it is.

I don't think there is a heaven because you all gets buried in the same sort of place. How on earth can you get out of a coffin and six feet of dirt and take a trip to the sky. I think it is just another thing to make you good.

I'd say heaven is just a fantasy to give people peace of mind when they die.

I don't think there is a heaven because if there was it would have to be a pretty big place to take all the good people who have died.

I'm not struck on saying there is a heaven. I think you come back to life again.

I think when I die I will come back as someone else and carry on like that. I don't believe in heaven and hell because millions of people are dying every day, and there wouldn't be enough room for us all, we would be meeting stone age men and so on.

Heaven is not like a city or such but something abstract like happiness, it's something which you look forward to when you die somewhere where worry strain or heartbreak etc. doesnt exist. I think heaven is not a place above the clouded that's for children to belive in. I belive heaven his in the person. Heaven is like God you cannot see it or tuch it but it is there.

I think that heaven is in the heart, not in the clouds or any other place because that is where the goodness will come from.

Oh! I believe that heaven is all around you, and not way up in the clouds. I also believe that it is part of the mind.

Heaven is where God is and he is all around us.

how Do I now theres a heaven or you I Dot think there a heaven.

To the above question I honestly have not got an answer to it.

realy none of us nos where we will go.

Nobody nose.

Harold Loukes. *Teenage Religion* (1961), 63-6

The above is reduced from a somewhat longer list of cases interspersed with comments. Each 'paragraph' represents the beginning of a separate comment. The spelling follows Loukes' original source materials.

7.2.3 Rebellion

I have questioned several such young men who had been at Ittoen for some time. 'When you came here your parents said you had been behaving badly. But now you seem to be a good man. Can you tell me at what time you changed thus?'

The typical answer was something like this, 'The thing I

least expected was that no one at Ittoen blamed me for the faults with which my family had always reproached me. Even when they did not openly blame me, I always felt their inward reproach and the home atmosphere gave me a ceaseless sense of oppression. I did not always want to sleep late in the morning, but I used to stay in bed because I dreaded seeing their unpleasant faces. I really did have a conscience and sometimes I would get up early and try to do some work, but they would sneer at me and make fun of me, so that I returned to my bad habits. When I was sent to Ittoen I had a feeling of strong resentment and was certain I could never endure staying in such a lonely place even for a few days. The strange thing was that after the first night my rebellious spirit died down under the gentle attitude of the Toban. What won my heart most of all was your remark, "I, too, am guilty of wrong-doing". To my ears, which had constantly had to listen to my own wrong-doing, your remark was enormously impressive. Furthermore, you never blamed me at all. Instead you blamed yourself. My rebellious feeling vanished. I slept peacefully the first night and woke to the sound of wooden clappers. I got up and worked at the sweeping and dusting like the others. Although my ankles ached a little during the sutra chanting at the morning service, I felt like a new man. The breakfast consisted merely of a mixture of rice barley and boiled vegetables. But it tasted very good indeed. Ittoen Tenko-san, *A New Road to Ancient Truth*, 65-6

On the Ittoen community cf 6.2.4. A 'Toban' is a director or leader in the community. A 'conversion' in these terms does not necessarily imply submission to the values assumed by the family of the young man in question. Indeed the family may find it impossible to understand the meaning of his new life, as is clear from a case elsewhere described at length (Ittoen Tenko-san, 97-103).

7.3   LATER MATURITY

While a certain type of religious decision or 'conversion' is particularly associated with adolescence (cf 7.2) this does not mean that the religious development of the individual is finished at latest by the age of twenty-five. Indeed in some cases the further development may be of greater consequence than the initial positioning of adolescence. Specially clear or concentrated cases of further development include Starbuck's cases of 'adult reconstruction' (*The Psychology of Religion*, 277-93) which take place in the late twenties in terms of 'a new insight . . . that becomes the basis for apperceiving essential elements in old doctrines' (cf 7.3.1.). Thouless has pointed out that quite distinct cases of adult conversion can be documented and offers examples of moral, intellectual and mystical conversion (*An Introduction to the Psychology of Religion*, 187-215). Jung writes of a general process of individual development during adult life which he terms 'individuation', and in which religious symbols and meanings often play a major role (see 'Individual Dream Symbolism in Relation to Alchemy' in *Psychology and Alchemy* (1967). Many eastern religions, in spite of their reverence for precocious saints, normally presuppose a lengthy period of training and growth before their real goal can be attained. The wider psychological bearings of two such systems has been brought out in Jung's 'Commentary on "The Secret of the Golden Flower" ' in *Alchemical Studies* (1967), and Giuseppe Tucci's *The Theory and Practice of the Mandala* (1969). All of these seem to satisfy the need to digest or come to terms with a variety of previous experience.

7.3.1 Adult reconstruction

The dark period has nearly passed for me. My beliefs are largely what they formerly were, and the reconstruction was perhaps not entirely independent of the influence of the old beliefs; but it does not rest on them as a foundation.

I have had a slow process of construction and extreme simplification of belief. My few religious tenets seem perfectly in harmony with natural law and rational ideas. I have not accepted again anything once completely discarded. I have simple beliefs, yet strong on a few fundamental points.

I find, what has proved itself more and more true all the time, that the positive beliefs that I have gradually worked out in the school of experience in freedom of thought are one in essence with the religious beliefs of my childhood, that had been taught in the first place in terms so simple that they seemed to have nothing profound about them.

I have come back to a firm belief in God as revealed by the Holy Spirit in Jesus Christ, but I cannot return to the traditional beliefs concerning inspiration, atonement, the person of Christ, election, etc.

The terms God, freedom, love and immortality have more meaning to me now than ever before, not so theoretical as a few years ago, but nearer and more real.
Starbuck. *The Psychology of Religion,* 278-9

Each paragraph represents a separate case, the first four being of men mostly aged thirty; and the fifth being a woman aged thirty who from twenty-four to twenty-nine was 'without a religion'.

7.3.2 Understanding prayer
Four years ago I stopped saying my prayers—and felt terribly guilty about it, especially when training young folk for Church Membership! (You will know what I mean if I anticipate by saying that I still don't say my prayers, but that for nearly twelve months now I haven't stopped praying during my waking life.) The real breakthrough began when I realised that I had far more in common with the honest agnostic than with the average Christian. It continued to a crucial point during a period of six months two years ago when my secretary's husband was dying of cancer. For once I could not avoid the problem by popping

in to see the patient occasionally and saying a few godly words. Every morning I had to face his wife (who turned out to be highly intelligent theologically) and questions about death, the hereafter, and prayer. By the time he died we were both agnostic about a personal consciousness outside this life, and our understanding of the nature of prayer had begun to mature.

The process of re-orientation and building up has been a tremendous time of release and joy and this side of the experience has given me a deep understanding of 'hot gospel' religion.

There are some chorus hymns that by a process of demythologising I can now sing with fervour! D. L. Edwards and J. A. T. Robinson. *The Honest to God Debate* (1963), 79

The text is a letter written to Dr Robinson (then Bishop of Woolwich) by a Free Church minister on reading the former's book *Honest To God*.

7.3.3 A dream

I come to a strange, solemn house—the 'House of the Gathering.' Many candles are burning in the background, arranged in a peculiar pattern with four points running upward. Outside, at the door of the house, an old man is posted. People are going in. They say nothing and stand motionless in order to collect themselves inwardly. The man at the door says of the visitors to the house, 'When they come out again they are cleansed.' I go into the house myself and find I can concentrate perfectly. Then a voice says: 'What you are doing is dangerous. Religion is not a tax to be paid so that you can rid yourself of the woman's image, for this image cannot be got rid of. Woe unto them who use religion as a substitute for the other side of the soul's life; they are in error and will be accursed. Religion is no substitute; it is to be added to the other activities of the soul as the ultimate completion. Out of the fulness of life shall you bring forth your religion; only then shall you be blessed!' While the last sentence is being spoken in ringing tones I hear distant music, simple chords on an organ. Something about it reminds me of Wagner's

Fire Music. As I leave the house I see a burning mountain and I feel: 'The fire that is not put out is a holy fire' (Shaw, *Saint Joan*). C. G. Jung. *Psychology and Religion: West and East* (1969), 35-6

In view of Jung's lengthy analysis of this dream it would be presumptuous to annotate it briefly. It is one of the later dreams of a long series dreamed by 'one of those scientifically minded intellectuals who would be simply amazed if anybody should saddle them with religious views of any kind', a Catholic by education but not by practice. That the dream has profound significance is obvious even without commentary. It is an advance on an earlier, more confused and partly ironic dream about religious institutions, and is followed, in Jung's account, by a dream about 'the world clock' said to have given the subject 'an impression of the most sublime harmony' and to have been a turning point in the patient's psychological development.

7.3.4 Final thoughts of General Tojo
'My father died on the twenty-sixth of December, my father-in-law on the twenty-ninth of December, and now I go on the twenty-third. It's really quite a coincidence, isn't it?

> The autumn day is dying,
> And I can hear a voice calling,
> On this, the anniversary of Father's death.'

'Did you say "autumn"?' I queried at this point.
'I had to make it autumn; otherwise it would not make a good *haiku*.

> Not a cloud is there to cross
> And darken my mind.
> And with a full heart
> I hurry on my journey West.

'This is an old one of mine. You know I am dying at a very opportune time. For one thing, I can tender my apologies to the people. Next, I am able to offer myself as a sacrifice to peace and become one stone in the foundation for the rebuilding of Japan. Thirdly, I can die in piece of mind because no trouble was brought upon the Emperor. . . . The most important thing is that through faith I can die and go to the Paradise of Amida-Butsu. Yes, truly, I believe that this is the best time for me to die. Last night, when the announcement was delivered, I felt very cheery at heart . . .' Shinsho Hanayama. *The Way of Deliverance, Three Years with the Condemned Japanese War Criminals* (1955), 253-4

Hanayama, who was Buddhist chaplain to the war criminals, describes how many of them managed to cope with the past and communicate some hope for the future to their relatives, before execution.

___

7.4 BASIC PSYCHOLOGICAL FACTS

Without being precise about the mechanism involved, students of religion have long recognised that the main factors conditioning the life of the individual, which we might call 'basic psychological facts', have been important in the formulation of religious ideas. Thus van der Leeuw refers to Freud and states boldly, 'To every man his mother is a goddess, just as his father is a god. In the history of religion this has resulted in two great groups—the religions of the *Father,* who dwells in heaven and begets and acts . . . and side by side with these the religions of the *Mother* living and giving birth in the Earth, in whose womb all process has both its beginning and its end.' (*Religion in Essence and Manifestation* (1964), 99). Virginity, fertility and motherhood are often inextricably linked in the many examples of 'the mother' to be found in the history of religions (cf van der Leeuw, 91-100, Bleeker, *The Sacred Bridge* (1963), 83-111 and Jung, *Symbols of Transformation* (1967), 207-73). That other gods are Parent and Father figures, in terms of whom various conflicts and their resolutions are played out, may also be agreed without necessarily accepting Freud's improbable account of the historical or even psychological origins of Hebrew monotheism (cf Freud's *Moses and Monotheism* (1939)). It is well known that sexual drive may be projected and sublimated in religious imagery (cf 3.4.5). Common human fears, of evil and of the unknown, of social isolation, and of death, may also be both reflected and resolved in religious terms. Indeed it would be very surprising if matters of such importance in the inner life of the individual did *not* figure in symbolic systems supposed by definition (as being 'religious') to refer to matters of fundamental importance. This simple phenomenon has been exploited with great ingenuity by Jung in his theory of the collective unconscious bearing the archetypes or recurrent symbols. See especially *The Archetypes and the Collective Unconscious* (1959). However, many of the symbolic associations in Jung's work seem to be extremely imaginative, not to say fanciful; and since each normal individual is presented with the same basic psychological situations and factors, there seems little reason to go beyond recognition of the importance of these in the context of a continuous but conscious human culture. For example, Jung's comparison of mandala forms is quite fascinating; but can some relationship between unity and duality, trinity and quarternity, be avoided, if a small number of important ideas are to be associated with each other in various ways, whether mentally or pictorially?

7.4.1 Father and mother in Gnosticism

Behold this fair body that was nurtured by her! [*At death*] she encloseth it and consumeth it and maketh it as if it had never existed. And all the kindly mysteries which she produces and tends as [*one tends*] a lamp with oil, eventually she turns on them with teeth of wrath. This is the Earth of the Parents. She raised up physical life and she is the Great Mother from Whom

all swarming creatures, burgeonings and increase proceeded and
by Whom they are maintained . . .

Thus the whole earth is a house : it is a great house in which
mysteries are kept and selected by test. It is an Egg of Life
[House of Life] for the Great Father . . .

There are those who delight in the Father and those who
delight in the Mother. E. S. Drower. *The Secret Adam, A Study
of Naṣoraean Gnosis* (Oxford 1960), 13-14

Mother and Father are projected here into a Gnostic cosmology.

7.4.2   The four persons of the Trinity

The God whom earth, and sea, and sky
Adore and laud and magnify,
Who o'er their threefold fabric reigns,
The Virgin's spotless womb contains.

The God whose will by moon and sun,
And all things, in due course, is done,
Is borne upon a maiden's breast,
By fullest heavenly grace possessed.

How blest that Mother, in whose shrine
The great Artificer Divine,
Whose hand contains the earth and sky,
Vouchsafed, as in his ark, to lie!

Blest is the message Gabriel brought,
Blest by the work the Spirit wrought;
For whom the great desire of earth
Took human flesh and human birth.

All honour, laud, and glory be,
O Jesu, virgin-born, to thee!
All glory, as is ever meet,
To Father and to Paraclete. *Amen.*

Shadler. *The Beauties of the Catholic Church*, 153

7.4.3   Fear of the apparitions

All these terrifying deities, witches, and demons around you—
fear them not, flee them not! They are but the benevolent
Buddhas and Bodhisattvas, changed in their outward aspect. In
you alone are the five wisdoms, the source of the benign spirits!
In you alone are the five poisons, the source of the angry spirits!
It is from your own mind therefore that all this has sprung.
What you see here is but the reflection of the contents of your
own mind in the mirror of the Void. If at this point you should
manage to understand that, the shock of this insight will stun
you, your subtle body will disperse into a rainbow, and you will
find yourself in paradise among the angels. Conze. *Buddhist
Scriptures*, 229 (quoting *The Tibetan Book of the Dead*)

This text refers to the intermediary state between births.

7.4.4   Fear of isolation and death

O Lord, my God, I call for help by day;
   I cry out in the night before thee.
Let my prayer come before thee,
   incline thy ear to my cry!

For my soul is full of troubles,
   and my life draws near to Sheol.
I am reckoned among those who go down to the Pit;
   I am a man who has no strength,
like one forsaken among the dead,
   like the slain that lie in the grave,
like those whom thou dost remember no more,
   for they are cut off from thy hand.
Thou hast put me in the depths of the Pit,
   in the regions dark and deep.
Thy wrath lies heavy upon me,
   and thou dost overwhelm me with all thy waves.

P

Thou hast caused my companions to shun me;
  thou hast made me a thing of horror to them.
I am shut in so that I cannot escape;
  my eye grows dim through sorrow.
Every day I call upon thee, O Lord;
  I spread out my hands to thee.
Dost thou work wonders for the dead?
  Do the shades rise up to praise thee?
Is thy steadfast love declared in the grave,
  or thy faithfulness in Abaddon?
Are thy wonders known in the darkness,
  or thy saving help in the land of forgetfulness?

Psalms lxxxviii, 1-12

7.4.5 The holy city

Then I saw a new heaven and a new earth, for the first heaven and the first earth had vanished, and there was no longer any sea. I saw the holy city, new Jerusalem, coming down out of heaven from God, made ready like a bride adorned for her husband. I heard a loud voice proclaiming from the throne: 'Now at last God has his dwelling among men! He will dwell among them and they shall be his people, and God himself will be with them. He will wipe every tear from their eyes; there shall be an end to death, and to mourning and crying and pain; for the old order has passed away!'

Then he who sat on the throne said, 'Behold! I am making all things new!' And he said to me, 'Write this down; for these words are trustworthy and true. Indeed,' he said, 'they are already fulfilled. For I am the Alpha and the Omega, the beginning and the end. A draught from the water-springs of life will be my free gift to the thirsty . . .'

Then one of the seven angels that held the seven bowls full of the seven last plagues came and spoke to me and said, 'Come, and I will show you the bride, the wife of the Lamb.' So in the Spirit he carried me away to a great high mountain, and showed me the holy city of Jerusalem coming down out of heaven from

God. It shone with the glory of God; it had the radiance of some priceless jewel, like a jasper, clear as crystal. It had a great high wall, with twelve gates, at which were twelve angels; and on the gates were inscribed the names of the twelve tribes of Israel. There were three gates to the east, three to the north, three to the south, and three to the west. The city wall had twelve foundation-stones, and on them were the names of the twelve apostles of the Lamb. Revelation xxi, 1-6, 9-14. Cf 2.4.4

7.4.6 The magic city

For example, monks, suppose a group of men came to a wild jungle covering five hundred leagues. There is a guide who is wise and learned, shrewd and mentally strong, who knows the difficult ways through the forest and who is to lead the company through it, on to the Isle of Jewels. The great band of men are tired out, anxious and afraid, and say, 'Master, guide, leader, we are tired out, anxious, afraid and not at peace. Let us go back. This wild jungle stretches away so far.' The guide, who is well-versed in skilful devices, sees that the men want to go back, and thinks as follows, 'This is no good. These poor men will never get to that Isle of Jewels.' Out of pity for them he makes use of a skilful device. He produces a magic city, one, two or three hundred leagues in extent, right in the middle of the forest. Then he says to the men, 'Do not be afraid, everybody. Do not go back. There is a large town. Let us rest there and you can do anything which you have to do. You may stay there and be at peace. Take a rest there. Then anyone who has reason to may go on to the great Isle of Jewels.'

Then, monks, the men who had arrived in the forest are struck with amazement and wonder, and think, 'We have got out of the wild jungle. Let us stay here and be at peace.' So, monks, these men go into the city produced by magic, thinking that they have arrived. Again, they think they have been saved. 'We are at rest; We are cooled,' they think.

And so when the guide perceives that they have rested, he causes the magic city to disappear, and when it has disappeared he says to those men, 'Come on, everybody, the great Isle of Jewels is just near here. As for this city, I produced it in order to give you a rest.' *The Lotus Sutra,* chapter 7, this passage newly translated by Mr Andrew Rawlinson and the Venerable K. Gnanatilaka. Cf 4.6.

Notes for the Introduction

1. Cf Hideo Kishimoto, 'An Operational Definition of Religion', *Numen* 8, 3 (December 1961), 236-240.

2. Cf Ugo Bianchi, *Probleme der Religionsgeschichte* (translated from Italian, Göttingen 1964), 5-6, where Bianchi criticises E. B. Tylor's definition for the same reason. Cf E. B. Tylor, *Primitive Culture, Researches into the Development of Mythology, Philosophy, Religion, Language, Art and Custom*, 2 Vols (1871), Vol 1, 424. On Tylor's work, cf also E. E. Evans-Pritchard, *Theories of Primitive Religion* (Oxford 1965).

3. Cf Kishimoto, 'An Operational Definition of Religion', and Helmut von Glasenapp, *Buddhism, A Non-theistic Religion* (1970), 35-47.

4. Cf Mircea Eliade, 'Methodological Remarks on the Study of Symbolism', in M. Eliade and J. M. Kitagawa, *The History of Religions* (Chicago 1959), 95. Eliade writes, 'And every religious act, by the simple fact that it is *religious,* is endowed with a meaning which, in the last instance, is "symbolic", since it refers to supernatural values or beings.' One might well query whether *every* religious act necessarily involves a view of the world which divides it into natural and supernatural spheres.

5. Kishimoto ('An Operational Definition of Religion', 239) argues that this is not a universal aspect of religious experience. As if to strengthen his argument he completely misunderstands what is usually meant by experience of 'the holy'. Holiness is a secondary element, he says, 'brought forth as a result of the activities of the religious life', and he states moreover that holiness

increases in refined groups and is not important in the religions of the common people. For western writers, following Rudolf Otto (*The Idea of the Holy* 1923), the experience of 'the holy' or 'the numinous' is an experience of something weird, terrible and fascinating, an experience indeed which one might argue to be more important in the religions of common people than among specialised and refined groups. Neither 'the holy' nor 'holiness' is a satisfactory common denominator of religion.

6. Cf E. Durkheim, *The Elementary Forms of the Religious Life* (1915), 47. Durkheim's definition was more complex than this (see note 8 below) but these phrases indicated what is specifically religious.

7. Cf Jean Daniélou, 'Phenomenology of Religions and Philosophy of Religion', in Eliade and Kitagawa, *The History of Religions*, 71.

8. Durkheim's definition is a clear example of this. In *The Elementary Forms of the Religious Life*, 47, he formulated: 'A religion is a unified system of beliefs and practices relative to sacred things, that is to say, things set apart and forbidden — beliefs and practices which unite, into one single community called a church, all those who adhere to them.' The definition should be taken in the whole context of Chapter I of his book, entitled 'Definition of Religious Phenomena and of Religion'. Both the definition and his overall approach are criticised in Evans-Pritchard's *Theories of Primitive Religion*.

9. Kishimoto, 'An Operational Definition of Religion', 240.

10. Kishimoto, 'An Operational Definition of Religion', 240.

11. Eliade, 'Methodological Remarks on the Study of Symbolism', 88.

12. Eg Robert N. Bellah, *Tokugawa Religion* (New York 1957), 6, where he writes, 'By religion, I mean, following Paul Tillich, man's attitudes and actions with respect to his ultimate concern.'

13. W. Brede Kristensen. *The Meaning of Religion* : *Lectures in the Phenomenology of Religion* (The Hague 1960), 14.

14. Wilfred Cantwell Smith, 'Comparative Religion : Whither

and Why?' in Eliade and Kitagawa, *The History of Religions,* 42. Cantwell Smith admits that there are difficulties with this principle. For a positive application of it, see page 33 above.

15. Cf Evans-Pritchard, 76-7, and S. Freud, *Moses and Monotheism* (1939).

16. For further discussion see the introductory comments to Parts 6 and 7.

17. Kristensen, *The Meaning of Religion,* 1-2.

18. C. J. Bleeker, *The Sacred Bridge* (Leiden 1963), 36.

19. It is necessary to be quite strict about this limitation of aim. C. J. Bleeker, similarly, while being interested in constant forms and recurrent types in religion, has emphasised the importance of the irreducible differences between religions. In this way he seems after all to have recognised the finality of specific historical cases of religion as being that to which the comparative study of religion ultimately refers (cf *The Sacred Bridge,* 30-2).

20. A clearcut example would be Ninian Smart's *Reasons and Faiths* (1958) which (among other things) attempts a comparative correlation of certain religious states and concepts.

21. Bleeker attempted to make a fresh start which avoided evolutionism, *The Sacred Bridge,* 16-24.

22. In the German translation 'nature' is rendered *'Wesen'* (cf the frequent translation of *Wesen* into English as 'essence' in such contexts).

23. Joachim Wach, *The Comparative Study of Religions* (Columbia 1958), 27.

24. Van der Leeuw, *Religion in Essence and Manifestation* (1964), 666-7.

25. Bianchi claimed that it is legitimate in the history of religion to make value judgements. He wrote, 'One can for example speak of a religious superiority of Islamic Arabia over pre-Islamic Arabia, at least with regard to those circles especially strongly gripped by the faith of Mecca. The judgement "superiority" has regard not only to a greater complexity and functionality . . . but it also contains a genuine value . . .'

(*Probleme der Religionsgeschichte*, 17). However, in so far as this judgement does contain 'a genuine value' it is surely more appropriate to say that it goes beyond the immediately appropriate methodology into the realms of genuine debate.

Note on the Presentation
of Sources

Footnotes, and the numeration of lines, verses, etc, have been
edited out. Technical terms have sometimes been omitted. A
word or phrase to complete the sense has occasionally been
added in square brackets, but most words in square brackets
were already in the source quoted. A few extracts were translated
by the present writer, ie except in cases where the source cited
is already in English or as indicated in the Acknowledgements.
References are given in full the first time and in the Bibliography,
but otherwise are abbreviated. References to *The Holy Bible,
Revised Standard Version* (for Jewish Bible/Old Testament
quotations) or to *The New English Bible* (for New Testament
quotations) are given simply by abbreviated book title, chapter
and verse. Where only the date of a publication is given, the
place of publication is London. Various cross-references have
been given from time to time but there are many more cases
where further examples of this or that detail are to be found
under other headings.

Bibliography

Ahmad, Khurshid (ed). *Studies in the Family Law of Islam* (Karachi 1961)

Arberry, Arthur J. *The Koran Interpreted,* two vols (1955) (Trans). *Discourses of Rūmī* (1961)

Argyle, Michael. *Religious Behaviour* (1958)

Aston, W. G. (trans). *Nihongi, Chronicles of Japan from the Earliest Times to A.D. 697* (1896, 1956)

Barrett, C. K. *The New Testament Background: Selected Documents* (1958)

Bellah, Robert N. *Tokugawa Religion, The Values of Pre-Industrial Japan* (New York 1957)

Berkowitz, M. I., Brandauer, F. P. and Reed, J. H. 'Folk Religion in an Urban Setting, A Study of Hakka Villagers in Transition', *Ching Feng* XII, 3-4 (Hong Kong 1969)

Bettenson, Henry. *Documents of the Christian Church* (1943)

Bianchi, Ugo. *Prolbleme der Religionsgeschichte* (trans from Italian, Göttingen 1964)

Birge, John Kingsley. *The Bektashi Order of Dervishes* (1965)

Bleeker, C. J. *The Sacred Bridge* (Leiden 1963)

Blyth, R. H. *Zen and Zen Classics* (Tokyo 1966)

Book of Common Prayer (1662)

Bright, John. *A History of Israel* (1960)

Broadhurst, J. R. C. (trans). *The Travels of Ibn Jubayr* (1952)

Brodie, Israel (ed). *The Authorised Daily Prayer Book of the United Hebrew Congregations of the British Commonwealth of Nations* (1962)

Carroll, Paul. *The Satirical Letters of St Jerome* (Chicago 1956)

Charles, R. H. *The Apocrypha and Pseudepigrapha of the Old Testament in English* (Oxford 1913)

China Pictorial (Peking, September 1968)

Cicero, Marcus Tullius (C. W. Keyes trans). *De Re Publica, De Legibus* (1928)

Conze, E. *Buddhist Scriptures* (Harmondsworth 1959)

Cox, Harvey. *The Secular City* (1965)

Daniélou, Jean. 'Phenomenology of Religions and Philosophy of Religion', in Eliade, M. and Kitagawa, J. M. (eds) *The History of Religions* (Chicago 1959)

Darmesteter, James (trans). *The Zend-Avesta, Part I, The Vendīdād*. Müller, Max (ed) Sacred Books of the East IV (1880, Delhi 1956)

Dator, James Allen. *The Soka Gakkai* (Washington 1969)

Dawson, Christopher. *The Historic Reality of Christian Culture* (New York 1960)

Dilworth-Harrison, T. *Every Boy's Confirmation Book* (1950)

Dods, Reith and Pratten (trans). *The Writings of Justin Martyr and Athenagoras* (Edinburgh 1867)

Drower, E. S. *The Secret Adam, A Study of Naṣoraean Gnosis* (Oxford 1960)

Dumoulin, Heinrich. *The History of Zen Buddhism* (1963)

Durkheim, E. *The Elementary Forms of the Religious Life* (1915)

Edwards, D. L. and Robinson, J. A. T. *The Honest to God Debate* (1963)

Eliade, Mircea. *From Primitives to Zen* (1963)
    'Methodological Remarks on the Study of Symbolism' in Eliade, M. and Kitagawa, J. M. listed below
    Patterns in Comparative Religion (1958)

Eliade, M. and Kitagawa, J. M. *The History of Religions* (Chicago 1959)

Engels, Friedrich. *Ludwig Feuerbach und der Ausgang der klassischen deutschen Philosophie* (1888, Berlin 1946)

Evans-Pritchard, E. E. *Theories of Primitive Religion* (Oxford 1965)

Firth, Raymond. *History and Traditions of Tikopia* (Wellington 1961)

Fiske, Adele. 'Religion and Buddhism Among India's New Buddhists', *Social Research*, 36, no 1 (Spring 1969), 123-157

Fremantle, Anne. *The Papal Encyclicals in Their Historical Context* (New York 1956)

Freud, S. *Moses and Monotheism* (1939)

Friedlander, Gerald (trans). *Laws and Customs of Israel, Compiled from the Codes Chayye Adam ('Life of Man') Kizzur Shulchan Aruch ('Condensed Code of Laws')* (1924)

Frör, Kurt (ed). *Das Zeichnen im Kirchlichen Unterricht* (München 1958)

Gaster, Theodor H. (trans). *The Dead Sea Scriptures* (New York 1956)

Geertz, Clifford. *The Religion of Java* (New York 1960)

Goldman, Ronald. *Religious Thinking from Childhood to Adolescence* (1963)

Gray, Robert F. *The Sonjo of Tanganyika, An Anthropological Study of an Irrigation-based Society* (1963)

Gropp, R. O. *Der dialektische Materialismus* (Leipzig 1961)

Gupta, Mahendranath. *The Gospel of Sri Ramakrishna* (New York 1969)

Hakeda, Yoshihito (trans). *The Awakening of Faith* (New York 1967)

Harton, F. P. *The Elements of the Spiritual Life: A Study in Ascetical Theology* (1932)

Hori, Ichiro. *Folk Religion in Japan, Continuity and Change* (Chicago 1968)

Horner, I. B. (trans). *Book of Discipline IV* (1951)

Isaacs, Nathan. *The Growth of Understanding in the Young Child* (1961)

Ittoen Tenko-san. *A New Road to Ancient Truth* (1969)

Jacobi, Hermann, *Jaina Sûtras Part II.* Müller, Max (ed) Sacred Books of the East XLV (Oxford 1895)

Jahoda, Gustav. *The Psychology of Superstition* (1969)
James, John. *A Comment upon the Collects* (1877)
James, William. *The Varieties of Religious Experience* (1952)
Jones, J. J. (trans). *The Mahāvastu* (3 vols, 1949, 1952 and 1956)
Jung, C. G. *Alchemical Studies* Collected Works 13 (1967)
    The Archtetypes and the Collective Unconscious Collected
      Works Vol 9, Part I (1959)
    Psychology and Alchemy Collected Works 12 (1967)
    Psychology and Religion : West and East Collected Works
      11 (1969)
    Symbols of Transformation Collected Works 5 (1967)
Kamstra, J. H. *Encounter or Syncretism* (Leiden 1967)
Kanamatsu, Kenyro. *Naturalness* (California 1956)
Kawasaki, Kashigumi and Masuda. *Toshijin no Shakaiteki
    Kinō* Vol 1 (Tokyo 1959)
Kern, H. (trans). *Saddharma-Puṇḍarīka or The Lotus of the
    True Law.* Müller, Max (ed) Sacred Books of the East XXI
    (1884, New York 1963)
Kishimoto, Hideo. 'An Operational Definition of Religion',
    Numen 8, no 3 (December 1961), 236-40
Kitch, M. J. *Capitalism and the Reformation* (1967)
Kristensen, W. Brede. *The Meaning of Religion : Lectures in
    the Phenomenology of Religion* (The Hague 1960)
Küng, Hans. *The Theologian and the Church* (1965)
Lake, Kirsopp (trans). *The Apostolic Fathers* The Loeb
    Classical Library (1965)
Lanternari, Vittorio. *The Religions of the Oppressed* (New York
    1965)
Lienhardt, G. *Divinity and Experience, The Religion of the
    Dinka* (Oxford 1961)
Ling, T. O. *A History of Religion East and West* (1968)
Loukes, Harold. *Teenage Religion* (1961)
Macauliffe, M. A. *The Sikh Religion* (Delhi 1963)
Mathur, K. S. 'The Meaning of Hinduism in Rural Malwa', in
    Viyarthi, L.P. (ed). *Aspects of Religion in Indian Society*
    (Meerut 1961)

Mao Tse-tung. *Quotations from Chairman Mao Tse-tung* (Peking 1966)

Marx, K. and Engels, F. *Manifesto of the Communist Party* (1848, Moscow 1952)

Maududi. Abul A'la. *The Meaning of the Quran* (Lahore 1967)

May, Jacques. *Candrakīrti Prasannapadā Madhyamakavṛtti* (Paris 1959)

Mcleod, W. H. *Gurū Nānak and the Sikh Religion* (Oxford 1968)

Mills, D. E. (trans). *A Collection of Tales from Uji* (Cambridge 1970)

Modi, J. J. *The Religious Ceremonies and Customs of the Parsees* (Bombay 1937)

Morgan, Kenneth W. (ed). *The Religion of the Hindus* (New York 1953)

Müller, Max (ed). *Sacred Books of the East* (see Darmesteter, Kern, Jacobi and Takakusu respectively)

The New English Bible, New Testament (Oxford and Cambridge 1961)

Ñyāṇamoli, Bhikkhu (trans). *The Path of Purification (Visuddhi-Magga) by Bhadantacariya Buddhaghosa* (Colombo 1964)

Otto, Rudolf. *The Idea of the Holy* (1923, 1959)

People's Mass Book (London, Dublin and Melbourne 1966)

Piaget, Jean. *The Psychology of Intelligence* (1950)

Pickthall, Mohammed Marmaduke. *The Meaning of the Glorious Koran* (New York, no date)

Polemos, Heft 14 (Basel, October 1970)

Raemers, W. (C.SS.R.). *Indulgenced Prayers* (Catholic Truth Society 1956)

Renondeau, G. *Le Shugendô: Histoire, Doctrine et Rites des Anachonètes dits Yamabushi*. Cahiers de la Société Asiatique 8 (Paris 1964)

Rhys Davids, T. W. and C. A. F. *Dialogues of the Buddha* Part II (1910, 1966), Part III (1921, 1965)

Rice, John R. (ed). *The Sword of the Lord, An Independent*

Christian Weekly (Murfreessboro, Tennessee, 3 September 1965 and 15 April 1966)

Richardson, Cyril C. (et al). *Early Christian Fathers.* Library of Christian Classics Vol I (1953)

Roberts, Nesta. 'Last Salute to a Great Soldier', *Guardian* (2 February 1967)

Robertson, Roland. *The Sociological Interpretation of Religion* (Oxford 1970)

Roth, Cecil (ed and trans). *The Haggadah* (1959)

Sale, George. *The Koran* (1734, 1899)

Sarma, D. S. 'The Nature and History of Hinduism,' in Morgan, Kenneth W. *The Religion of the Hindus* (New York 1953)

Shadler, F. J. (trans). *The Beauties of the Catholic Church : or, Her Festivals, and Her Rites and Ceremonies, Popularly Explained* (New York 1881)

Sheldon, W. H. *The Varieties of Temperament* (New York 1942)

Siddiqi, M. Abdul Hamid. *Prayers of the Prophet (Masnūn Du'a'ain)* (Lahore 1968)

Singh, Indera P. 'Religion in Daleke, a Sikh Village', in Viyarthi, L. P. (ed), *Aspects of Religion in Indian Society* (Meerut 1961)

Smart, Ninian. 'Interpretation and Mystical Experience', *Religious Studies* I (1965), 75-87

  The Phenomenon of Religion (1972)

  Reasons and Faiths (1958)

  The Religious Experience of Mankind (1971)

Smith, Joseph. *Joseph Smith's Testimony* (Church of Jesus Christ of Latter Day Saints, pamphlet, no date)

Smith, Wilfred Cantwell. 'Comparative Religion : Whither and Why?' in Eliade, M. and Kitagawa, J. M. *The History of Religions* (Chicago 1959)

Spinks, G. Stephens. *Psychology and Religion* (1963)

Spiro, Melford E. *Burmese Supernaturalism, A Study in the Explanation and Reduction of Suffering* (Englewood Cliffs 1967)

Stagner, Ross. *Psychology of Personality* (New York 1965)

Starbuck, Edwin Diller. *The Psychology of Religion, An Empirical Study of the Growth of Religious Consciousness* (1901)

St Thomas Aquinas (by an anonymous member of the Dominican Order) (Catholic Truth Society 1948)

Suzuki, Daisetz Teitaro. *Mysticism Christian and Buddhist* (1957)

The Training of the Zen Buddhist Monk (New York 1965)

Takakusu, J. (trans). The Amitâyur-Dhyâna-Sûtra' in Cowell, E. B., Müller, Max and Takakusu, J. *Buddhist Mahâyâna Sûtras*. Müller (ed) Sacred Books of the East XLIX (Oxford 1894)

Tenrikyo Kyokai Honbu (ie Tenrikyo Church Head Office). *A Short History of Tenrikyo* (Tenri 1967)

The Holy Bible, Revised Standard Version (New York 1952)

The Methodist Hymn-book (1904)

The Tanni Shō, Notes Lamenting Differences. Ryukoku Translation Series II (Kyoto 1963)

Thomas, D. Winton (ed). *Documents from Old Testament Times* (1958)

Thomas, Edward J. *The History of Buddhist Thought* (1951)

Thomsen, Harry. *The New Religions of Japan* (Rutland, Vermont 1963)

Thouless, R. H. *An Introduction to the Psychology of Religion* (Cambridge 1923, completely revised edition 1971, too late to be consulted)

Tissidatto, Ven Phra Maha Vichitr. *Buddhist Holy Days* (1966)

Tsunoda, R. (ed). *Sources of Japanese Tradition* (New York 1958)

Tucci, Giuseppe. *The Theory and Practice of the Mandala* (1969)

Tylor, E. B. *Primitive Culture, Researches into the Development of Mythology, Philosophy, Religion, Language, Art and Custom*, 2 vols (1871)

Underhill, Evelyn. *Mysticism, A Study in the Nature and Development of Man's Spiritual Consciousness* (1911)

Van der Leeuw, G. *Religion in Essence and Manifestation* (1964)

Van Gennep, Arnold. *The Rites of Passage* (1908, Chicago 1960)

Viyarthi (see Mathur and Singh respectively)

Von Glasenapp, Helmut. *Buddhism, A Non-theistic Religion* (1970)

Wach, Joachim. *The Comparative Study of Religions* (New York 1958)

Sociology of Religion (Chicago 1944)

Ware, James R. (trans). *The Sayings of Confucius* (New York 1955)

Weber, Max. *The Protestant Ethic and the Spirit of Capitalism* (1930)

Welch, Holmes. *The Practice of Chinese Buddhism 1900-1950* (Cambridge Mass. 1967)

Wilkens, Hermann, 'Kindersegnung oder Säuglingstaufe?', *Stimme der Gemeinde* 15 March 1971 (Frankfurt am Main)

Woods, James Haughton (trans). *The Yoga-system of Patañjali.* Harvard Oriental Series XVII (1914, Delhi 1966)

Woodward, F. L. (trans). *The Minor Anthologies of the Pali Canon.* Part II (1948)

World Union VIII, no 2 (Pondicherry April 1968)

World Union (pamphlet, Pondicherry 1968)

Worsley, Peter. *The Trumpet Shall Sound, A Study of 'Cargo' Cults in Melanesia* (1957)

Wright, David (trans). *Beowulf* (Harmondsworth 1957)

Yampolsky, Philip B. (trans). *The Platform Sutra of the Sixth Patriarch* (New York 1967)

Yearly Meeting 1921. *Christian Life Faith and Thought in the Society of Friends* (1922)

Zaehner, R. C. (trans etc). *The Bhagavad-Gītā* (Oxford 1969)

Concordant Discord, The Interdependence of Faiths (Oxford 1971)

(Trans). *Hindu Scriptures* (1966)

Hinduism (Oxford 1962)

Mysticism Sacred and Profane (Oxford 1961)

Zhong, Zi Mang. *Fei Dao Tien An Men Qu* (Peking 1966)

Acknowledgements

Certain books have been especially helpful to me, as will have been clear by the references to them, and this includes those which have been criticised for this or that reason. I should like to thank Mr Andrew Rawlinson and the Venerable K. Gnanatilaka who translated extract 7.4.6 from the Sanskrit, and Mrs Ling Thompson, who helped me with the translation of extract 1.1.6. I hesitate to implicate my colleagues in the Department of Religious Studies at the University of Lancaster, but I am grateful for their educational influence, comments and practical help, which at least reduced the number of imperfections somewhat.

Michael Pye

Index

Some references to major religions refer to extracts in which the term itself (Islam, Shinto, etc) does not specifically occur.